ROIN
IOPE
, Kenny

Mary Kenny is a leading journalist, writer and broadcaster, respected in the UK and Ireland alike. A senior writer for *The Express* in London, she also writes for the *Irish Independent* magazine and *The Irish Catholic*, and contributes to *The Spectator* and *The Tablet*. Throughout her life she has courted controversy, and has previously written books on the subjects of feminism, religion and abortion. Her most recent book, the highly-acclaimed *Goodbye to Catholic Ireland*, was published in 1997 and will be reissued in a revised edition by New Island in 2000. Mary is married with two sons and lives in both Ireland and England.

death by *heroin*
recovery by *hope*

Mary Kenny

**NEW
ISLAND**

DEATH BY HEROIN,
RECOVERY BY HOPE
First published November 1999 by
New Island Books
2 Brookside
Dundrum Road
Dublin 14
Ireland

1 3 5 7 9 10 8 6 4 2

Copyright © 1999 Mary Kenny

ISBN 1 902602 11 0

The Arts Council
An Chomhairle Ealaíon

New Island Books receives financial assistance from The Arts
Council (An Chomhairle Ealaíon), Dublin, Ireland.

Cover design: Slick Fish Design
Typesetting: New Island Books
Printed by Cox & Wyman, Reading

Contents

In loving memory of Conor Kenny
(1962-1998)
and Patrick Kenny
(1969-1998).
Always cherished by their family
and friends.

Preface and Acknowledgements

Because I regard myself as living between Ireland and England (I am a resident of the UK, but I spend a lot of time in Ireland) I have drawn on both Irish and British sources in researching this book. This has turned out to be helpful, because while the individual involved in heroin use and heroin dependency can be of any nationality, class, colour, religion or sex, I found certain variations in the approach to treatment in these different societies. Britain and Ireland differ in that it is legal to prescribe diamorphine (medicalised heroin) in certain restricted circumstances in the UK, but not in the Irish Republic. So it has been useful to compare and contrast attitudes to treatment, though I should emphasise that this undertaking is very far from being definitive, and there are many more specialists and clinics I would like to have seen, but time did not allow. I am no expert in this field; merely a reporter on a quest to make sense of a dreadful tragedy.

People have been very kind and helpful to me, and I would first of all like to thank the heroin users, recovering or struggling, who shared so generously of their experiences and indeed were very supportive of the project: heroin users *want* others to understand how they became drawn into the habit. Where I have used first names only, in the tradition of Narcotics Anonymous, I am respecting the anonymity of the individual. Where I have used both names, and where the addict is deceased, these are actual names.

My thanks to all those mentioned in the text, and to many others who gave me helpful background information, especially Tracey from Wales, Michael residing at Her Majesty's pleasure, Jim, Gavin, Thomas, Miriam, brave Caroline, Tom the musician, Paul from Kildare, Guy, Annie, Ron and Lynette. Thanks even to those I didn't get to meet and those who didn't show up: I appreciated their telephone messages and good intentions.

Thanks to Andrew for providing so much helpful background on pharmaceutical drugs, and to Ruth for being such a star.

I would especially like to thank three bereaved mothers who shared the experience of death by heroin with me: Annette Rodgers in Derby, Vicky Remnant in East Anglia and Mary Gaffney in Tallaght, Dublin. I learned so much from my conversations with them and felt touched by their courage. I would also like to thank Roger Johansen, a bereaved parent in slightly different circumstances, but whose insights were very helpful indeed, and who was especially kind to me.

I would like to acknowledge the specialists in drug treatment who agreed to interviews and gave me of their time and expertise. Thanks to Mary O'Shea, Assistant Director of The Merchant's Quay Project in Dublin. This excellent facility, founded by the Franciscan Sean Cassin in 1989 has as its central philosophy the duty of respect towards the addict. An addict should not be rebuffed by society, but respected as a person, and the Merchant's Quay Project runs many free of charge supportive services for addicts. I would also like to thank Celia and

Paul, and all at the family group at Merchant's Quay, who allowed me to attend an inspirational meeting for parents and family members of addicts.

I owe a special debt of gratitude to Maura Russell of the Rutland Centre in Templeogue, for her wise insights and knowledgeable guidance. In England, Diana Wells and Pauline Bissett at Broadway Lodge in Weston-super-Mare, Michael Audreson of the Rivendell Clinic at Oxford Street, London and Dr Adrian Garfoot, at the special charity trust clinic in the East End, the Laybourne, have been very helpful in sharing their considerable experience. Thanks, too, to Dr Bill Shanahan of the Brent, Kensington & Chelsea and Westminster Mental Health Trust, and to Dr Colin Brewer of the Stapleford Clinic in Belgravia.

I would like to thank Dr Margaret Bourke of Dublin, who explained to me much about the social profile of heroin users, and about the treatment clinics. She was not Patrick Kenny's doctor, and did not treat him, because of a family connection, but she understood the background to the case.

I would specially like to thank Dr John O'Connor, Consultant Psychiatrist and Director of Clinical Practice at the National Drug Treatment Centre at Trinity Court, Dublin. He supplied me with a collection of medical papers which were most valuable, and he was kind enough to read this manuscript and to say it was a good and a useful work.

There is an outstanding specialist library in London, the Institute for the Study of Drug Dependency, which acts as an archive for everything published about a wide range of drugs, and I should like to thank the librarian,

Stephan Schulte-Naering and his staff for their assistance and expertise.

I am grateful for an interview with the Dublin Coroner, Dr Brian Farrell. I thank the Coroner's office manager, Brian Hanney for showing me the melancholy archives of sudden deaths in Dublin, so many of which in recent years refer to death by drugs.

I thank Dr Farrell for introducing me to the research work of Mr Ray Byrne. Mr Byrne's academic thesis "The Relative Mortality Risks of Methadone and Other Drugs, implicated in Drug Related Deaths investigated by the Dublin City Coroner in 1998" was carried out for a primary degree in social care. This meticulously researched text showed that people who have taken methadone were at least twice as likely to have methadone implicated in their deaths than people who took heroin had heroin implicated in their deaths, thereby underlining how dangerous a drug methadone can be.

My special thanks to Grainne Kenny of EURAD: her short, readable leaflets on all the major drugs being used and abused are among the best and most accessible drug education sources. Thanks to Joe Anderson of Tallaght, who produces "The Shrew" and to Mike Goodman at Release in London. I have much appreciated a conversation with Will Self, the writer, on the subject of addiction and society. I would like to thank Joe Barnes for his helpful suggestions about amendments. Joe Joyce has been a patient, thorough and insightful editor of this book.

Thanks to Edward West, for reading background material for me, and for Patrick West for accessing material via the Internet. Gratitude to my husband

Richard West for being staunchly supportive of a project which made all around so miserable, at times. My thanks to my sister Ursula Kenny for American material.

My very special thanks to my niece Marie-Louise Kenny, gifted and wise beyond her years.

My sister-in-law, May, and my younger niece, Sarah, have asked me to make it clear that they wish to be dissociated from the publication of the first chapter of this book, as they feel it is an invasion of their privacy and an invasion of the privacy of both Patrick and Conor Kenny.

I greatly regret the distress this causes May and Sarah, both such gentle and dignified people. The book was nearing completion when it became obvious that this would be the case. It is not my intention to invade my nephews' privacy, which I feel was already invaded by a public inquest and a coroner's report; my intention is to celebrate their lives, and to show how irreparable a loss death from heroin can be.

My colleague Peter Hitchens said to me "If this book saves one other life, it is worth doing." I ardently hope that it may do so.

The poem, 'Lady Heroin', which appears on page 76 was composed by a prisoner signed only "Anon". It was passed to me by Annette Rodgers. If authorship can be established, we would be glad to acknowledge it in any subsequent editions of this book.

The prose-poem How to Help an Addict, By an Addict, was composed by me, but inspired by a conversation with an experienced and compassionate person from Narcotics Anonymous, Margaret.

Half the revenue from this book will go to the Aislinn Treatment Centre (for young people and their families) at

Ballyraggett, Co Kilkenny. A donation will be made to Eurad, the drugs education and family intervention charity. These accounts can be publicly audited through the publisher's records.

Part I

Introduction

You may think you love your lover,
  but the drug is stronger.
You may think you love your mother,
  but the drug is stronger.
You may think you love your father, brother,
  sister, child, but, be assured,
    the drug is stronger.

—M.K.

This is not an easy story for me to write. I recoil from writing it at all. It is painful to set out these melancholy events, and to subject my bereaved family to the recollection of what has been. But it is a necessary story for me to record, and I think, for others who may be afflicted by the heroin experience.

It is a necessary requiem for two young men, who are as alive in my imagination as I am myself, who were full of personality, funny, intelligent and endearing; who had remarkably nice parents, were unequivocally loved, and had attended one of the best private schools in Dublin. Two young men who might have had a lifetime of potential ahead of them. And yet their fate was death by heroin, in December 1998, just three weeks apart.

This is a necessary story, but a terrible story.

When their inquest was carried out in the Dublin Coroner's Court, in June 1999, the State pathologist Dr

15

Marie Cassidy remarked ruefully: "I suppose this will just be another statistic about heroin deaths tucked away in the corner of a newspaper." She is accustomed to the brief news references to death by heroin in Dublin, and is dismayed by the number of healthy young corpses she is obliged to examine, healthy in every respect except that opiate drugs have brought these lives to an end.

And, indeed, a short, depressing news report appeared reflecting the bare facts. "Two brothers die of heroin overdoses," ran the headline of a downpage report in the *Irish Independent*. "Heroin claimed the lives of two Dublin brothers in the same month last year, inquests into their deaths were told yesterday." Conor Kenny, aged thirty-six, found dead in a hotel bathroom, a syringe and other drugs equipment near his body. Patrick Kenny, aged twenty-nine, found dead in his apartment at the South Circular Road, on Christmas Day. The bare facts were repeated again in the following Sunday newspaper. Later in the summer of 1999, the current affairs magazine *Magill* ran a report which again reiterated these stark facts, in more detail describing how Conor's body had lain dead all night, for a full ten hours, before it was discovered.

All heroin deaths, when subjected to the unsparing description of a news report, or a coroner's record, seem squalid. A newspaper reader will see it, and turn the page, perhaps even dismissively. How little do these cold facts reveal the warm lives behind the disinterested evidence. How little do they explain the person, the background, the reasons why ....

Dr Cassidy, a young woman herself, and a Scot, said that she wished that the media would write longer articles, and that both the media and the public at large would take much more seriously this affliction of drug deaths among young people. While remaining professionally cool, there was a gritted anger in her expression. It should be a priority to warn, to make it known, that you can just take a hit from heroin, and die. It doesn't have to be "bad" heroin. It can be any heroin. Heroin depresses the respiratory system. You breathe out and you never breathe in again, though you may be otherwise young and healthy and strong. There should be a serious campaign about it, not just little squibs in the corners of the papers.

The Dublin Coroner, Dr Brian Farrell, spoke of "the silent epidemic" of those young people dying from drug use in Ireland today, and, at the end of the inquest, altered the register of his voice from that of the impartial public servant, to that of a distressed sympathiser and empathic parent. Three times, he reiterated his condolences, so affected did he feel for the double family death whose harrowing details he had presided over. "I do not know how a family can recover from this," he said, sadly. I do not quite know either. There have been other Dublin families which have lost two brothers, but no family that I could trace in the Coroner's recent records where there were no other sons left. Their deaths were not unusual, but the circumstances were unique.

It is necessary to record and archive Conor and Patrick's lives, which were gifted but unrealised because of the drug; it is necessary to undertake the quest to understand why people use heroin — Dublin alone is said to have 13,000 heroin addicts. It is also necessary to say that death's claim is not inevitable. There is recovery. But it must be actively pursued and communally supported. There must also be knowledge. Heroin must be spoken of as openly as we speak of wine, so that we may understand it.

Some weeks after my nephews' deaths, I talked to a young Dubliner, Joe, who had got clean after "years and years" on heroin, often topped up with alcohol. He was a lad from the inner city, and he had trawled the depths: twice he had been admitted to hospital in an apparently moribund state, and once actually pronounced dead. He had been, he said, completely in the gutter before he started his recovery.

"How — and why — did you give up the habit?" I asked him. His answer came, in a way, as a chilling reproach.

"I had an aunt who helped me," he said. "She gave me hope. You must have hope to have recovery."

I was Conor and Patrick's aunt. I didn't help them enough. Perhaps I didn't know how to.

It is necessary now to transmit to others what I have learned about death by heroin, and recovery by hope.

Chapter One

Death by Heroin — a Family Tragedy

All life is suffering.
— Buddhist saying.

I see your faces now before me, my darling nephews, as I always will do. Conor: such a clever, witty, big face: intelligent, laughing, jocular: one never knew whether he was codding or not. Patrick, whom Conor sometimes called PK, to distinguish between the two Patricks in the family, Patrick Kenny and my son Patrick West. PK, with a fine, shy, sensitive face, pale and dreamy — a sweet person, and as I learned too late, a vulnerable person who bravely tried to hide that vulnerability. My father's eyes were replicated in PK's. My father, his grandfather, was also Patrick Kenny: I now look at the picture of my father, as a young man, and wonder if there was a family weakness there which foretold the tragedy. Was there an "addiction gene" in the Kennys? A tragedy changes the past as well as the future, because you look in the past for clues of what was later to unfold.

I knew that Conor was "experimenting" with drugs, because I had been told by his sister Marie-Louise, who was passionately, and rightly, opposed to this dabbling. And the last time I saw Conor, which would have been in November 1998, his conversation was so jerky, so liable to flit from one subject to another, so hyper-hyper, that even I, inexperienced in the drug culture, concluded that he must be using cocaine. But I am now told that this was not the case. He certainly used cannabis since his late teens. And he might have used ecstasy, as millions do.

And yet I didn't take the notion — that he might be using a range of drugs — particularly seriously. It simply never crossed my mind that any harm would come to Conor. He was strong, he was indomitable, he seemed, in Marie-Louise's words, indestructible. Cocaine, which I wrongly thought the prime suspect, is, according to my younger colleagues in the media quite "cool". People did it at weekends and that was okay. Did it make your food come out your nose, after it had destroyed the mucous lining? No, that was just tabloid hysteria. Cannabis, ecstasy, coke — chill out, get real, only fogeys get into a sweat about these ....

Then it was intimated to me, too, that Conor was latterly using heroin. Marie-Louise was extremely concerned about this over the previous twelve months, but I said he'd probably get over it. I may even have told her that she shouldn't fret so much about her brothers. They had their own lives to live. And people in their thirties don't suddenly become addicts, surely. Conor was just going through a phase.

I had become aware, over the past few years, that PK had a heroin problem. It had been an immense cross to his widowed mother, who had herself been to a counsellor about it, and who prayed ardently that he might get help to quit the habit. I knew she had done everything in her power to get him to stop, and I thought, in that airey, everything-will-work-itself-out way, that the situation was improving. Yet of course, Patrick was a worry. But Conor, the older brother, he was different. He wasn't a worry. Conor was motivated. Conor was in control. He had travelled all over former Yugoslavia, on a shoe-string, filming. According to a colleague, he had acted with daring and courage in a war zone.

Conor was a talented film-maker. He was an artist. He had a madcap streak. But I never imagined that Conor was in any serious danger. He was also obsessed with his work, with achieving something in film. I have always believed that individuals who have a strong sense of purpose in life, a strong vocational ambition, will not be destroyed by a drug.

Motivation is everything, in my experience. If you are motivated to do something with your life, you do it. If you have work to do, you have a strong instinct to survive until it is done. Read Conor Cruise O'Brien's famous, even hilarious, essay on Yeats in *Passion and Cunning*. The poet Yeats got deeply involved in Irish nationalism — but only insofar as it served the work. When any question of danger loomed, the work gene was activated, as it were, reminding the unconscious mind that for the work to be accomplished, the life must first be preserved. I believed that our Conor's passion for film would always see him through.

Conor Kenny ate, drank, walked, talked, slept film. He had won an award at the Galway Arts Festival in 1993 for a short film; and a documentary he had made about the former Yugoslavia, *Journey to Mostar*, had been shown to acclaim on RTE. He made the Mostar film on the ingenuity of his own endeavours, and he was just about to shoot a sequel. On the day he died, he was celebrating, with effervescent happiness, a commission he had just received to do another Balkan movie.

21

Conor, I thought, would never do anything crazy — at least no more than the rest of us, for hadn't I, and so many of my contemporaries, drunk Dublin dry during our misspent youth? Hadn't we all been reckless and heedless in our time? But not so reckless and heedless as to die before our time.

It never crossed my mind that a drug could kill Conor. I repeat this to underline it. I never thought about it, once. He might slide into a bad habit. He might need to sober up, and cut down on excess. People do that. People get sense in middle age.

What I didn't know, what people don't in general think about, is that with a drug habit, you don't always have the time to acquire the sense of middle age. The drug kills before you can tackle it. Candy is dandy, but liquor is quicker, wrote Ogden Nash: but heroin is quicker still, to grip, to hold, to destroy. Those who insouciantly compare a quick shot of heroin with a quick shot of whiskey forget to add that those who die from too much whiskey are generally in their 60s, 70s, 80s. I've known old soaks to perish from alcohol: and that's just what they were — old. Heroin kills those in their 20s and 30s. There is a big difference, not just for those it kills, but for those it leaves behind.

As Conor's sister, Marie-Louise, wrote in a moving article in the *Sunday Independent* some weeks after the bereavement: "Heroin destroys lives. Not only the lives of the people who take it, but the future of those who are left behind." When older people die, it is the past that we lose. When younger people perish, it is the future that is changed, for them, and for their family, friends, and contemporaries.

*

All through November 1998, I was dogged by an unusual headache. It was located on one side of my head only and concentrated on the temple. I am easily alarmed by health worries and I prepared myself for the onset of a terminal illness. This put me in a morbid mood, and on December 1, driving from Kent to London, I had a macabre experience which gave me the graveyard blues.

I know this road well, because I take it regularly, and yet, on this occasion, I unexpectedly missed an exit. This was to bring me into London via the East End, rather than through the serpentine suburbs of the south side of the city. As I drove along the Commercial Road, in Whitechapel, I saw before me, a horse-drawn hearse, which struck me initially as rather fetching.

The horses were black, and plumed. The hearse was Victorian or Edwardian, with engraved glass. It is a handsome and theatrical sight, a horse-drawn hearse. It is a filmic sight. I'd like that for my funeral, I thought. So Joycean. (In the East End of London, as it happens, it sometimes denotes a gangster's stylish send-off.) And then as I came closer, I saw that the name of the deceased was spelled out in flowers. "MARY", it said. I do not like to live by superstitions, but that, I thought, was very like an omen. It felt unlucky.

That night I struggled with sleeplessness, and then dreamed I was in the presence of the Angel of Death, his great wings flapping as he came to seek me. The headache grew worse. Yet the following was a routine day: I went to the office, I wrote a book review, and I had supper with two friends at the Reform Club.

When I got back to the house, I learned then that it was not for me, yet, that the Angel of Death had come.

"Sit down, Mum. It's bad news." My own sons had red eyes.

Oh, what in God's name ...

"It's Conor."

"Conor?"

Silence.

"Dead?"

Silence.

Yes, he was. Dead. Laughing, jousting, joking Conor. Found dead in a Dublin hotel. He had had a pint, gone into the toilet and died.

I couldn't believe it, and yet, I could. The Angel of Death hovered. I sat down.

Poor Conor: his big, child's face, still. His talent, his dreams, his ambitions all halted in a night. Did he know as he died? Had he suffered? My sister in New York, Ursula, couldn't bear to think of him perhaps lying there, all night, dying ...

The initial cause of death was given as cardiac arrest. His death had been immediate. But there was a suspicion that a "recreational" drug was involved.

His brother Patrick left a fragment of an account which painfully describes how this December day had been for him. "Today, at approx 2.00 p.m. I had the misfortune to call out to my mother's house in Booterstown," he wrote on December 2. He had recently moved into a new flat, and he wanted to "collect some bits and pieces for my new abode. As I got on the Number 45 bus I thought briefly about my brother, to whom I have always been very close, and I thought that it would be very nice to go for a pint with him.

"Anyhow I arrived out at my mother's to find no one at home. However, I set about making myself something to eat whilst I waited.

About twenty mins after I arrived, my mother arrived home and I got the impression that she was quite glad to see me. We began to chat and she told me that my brother Conor was somewhat annoyed with me as I had taken four of his wine glasses, to which I simply laughed. Then she informed me that he had just bought a new 'Ready-to-go' phone, at which stage I remembered the last time he had gotten a mobile phone was about two-and-a-half years ago, for a film that he was originally producing called *Separation Anxiety*."

Patrick went on to recollect how much Conor — like his father James before him — enjoyed a new gadget. He imagined Conor taking pleasure in acquiring the new mobile phone, and how they would talk about it together later.

"So it's 2.00 p.m. on Wednesday 2/12/98 and me and Mammy are chatting about this and that when there is a ring on our front door bell. I immediately assumed it was Conor, that he had no keys. Anyway, Mammy says she will go and answer it and as she opens the first door, she shouted back to me that there are two people at the door whom she has never seen before. [The outer door is glass.] I can tell that there is a great deal of fear in her voice.

As she opens the front door I position myself so as I can hear what is being said. I immediately sussed that something was amiss. Then I heard them saying they were dicks and if we knew Conor Kenny. Because a young man with the name Conor

Kenny on him had been found dead in the Central Hotel. Firstly I tried to convince myself that they were mistaken, even though I knew full well that it was my lovely brother that they were talking about."

In that dreadful moment was PK's own death, three weeks later, also foretold? One can only imagine the pain, the shock, the despair, the wretchedness of that moment for him. The younger brother had ever been the older's lieutenant. Their father, my late brother, had often remarked, with pleasure, on PK's dedication to Conor.

The State Laboratory reported six months later that Conor's blood and urine contained a fatal dose of free morphine: heroin is broken down into morphine in the body. A moderate amount of alcohol was also present, which was not considered to have played any significant part in his death.

Conor was not a heroin addict, but he had been using it recreationally, mostly through smoking. The State Pathologist reported that there were no tracks on his arms or elsewhere which would indicate a history of injecting. It is likely that he had progressed, as heroin users will do, at some stage over the previous year from recreational smoking to injection (which provides a quicker high.) There were no reports that this was a batch of "bad" heroin around Dublin at the time. It was, from all that could be told, a normal heroin hit. But a "normal" heroin hit can kill.

The days after a sudden family death pass in a frozen haze. Denial and disbelief are the initial reactions. I was in Dublin. I had a business lunch which I fulfilled, but three-quarters of the way through, I just wanted it to be over. I just wanted to get away from the artificiality of the restaurant setting, to talk to the family, to be alone too. The knowledge of his death would recede in waves, and then return again effusively. Gradually, the consciousness of it filled the room, and seeped into everything, and then everything in Dublin seemed to be attached to his ghost. I saw him everywhere, and saw him many times over, taking the shape of other men, in the street. A male seen from the back would suddenly be Conor, and then turn round, and it would all dissolve. He might have done this as a film: dissolve.

I don't want this to be about me. The loss of my nephew was a lesser bereavement to me than it was to his afflicted mother, his brother, his two sisters, who were prostrated with grief — and also with disbelief. An aunt is one degree of kinship removed. Yet this is how I experienced it. And what I experienced was that a heroin death has an unforgettable effect on the whole family, and on many friends.

Because it didn't have to happen. The laboratory report of a drug-linked death is so horribly poignant because it emphasises, in its clinical way, that the deceased was in the best of health. "The scalp, skull and meninges were healthy. The brain weighed 1595 gm. and showed no abnormality ... The vessels at the base of the brain were patent and healthy ... the coronary arteries, healthy; the cardiac valves, healthy, the gastric mucosa, healthy ... the small and large intestines, normal, the liver normal, the spleen, normal, the gallbladder, pancreas and adrenal glands healthy, the kidneys, normal ...."

*

A funeral took place, two days later, after the body was released from the post-mortem. A post-mortem, that is a medical examination of the remains, must be done where there are unusual or suspicious circumstances, but the coroner's court inquest, in which post-mortem details are put into the public realm, may not occur, in Ireland, for several months.

But Irish funerals usually take place quickly, and everyone is thrown into a flurry of activity, of arrangements about comings and goings, cars, food, wine, burials, graveyard.

There is, before the funeral itself, the *ceremonie des adieux*. This is the viewing of the corpse in the funeral parlour, the farewells, the leave-taking. Conor's mother, May, bravely did that, though it was a terrible thing to have to do, to view her first-born, lying there in his coffin. What torments mothers have to bear, in grief.

I thought of the day that Conor was born, in September 1962, and then, how proud my brother James had been when he brought the baby home from hospital. I was a teenager, and I think I was jealous of the attention given to this infant. So much fuss was made of him, the first child in the family since 1944, the first grandchild on both sides. Oh, the billing and cooing over the little bundle. Conor was wanted, cherished, adored.

"People who become dependent on heroin and other heavy-end drugs," says a standard textbook used in drug education written by Melanie McFadyean, "have almost always suffered an emotional drama early in their lives which has never been resolved." Sexual abuse is quickly in the frame. Dr John O'Connor, of the National Drug Treatment Centre in Dublin claims that among heroin users, sexual abuse is "prevalent". Clinical depression is present among a quarter of heroin users. Homelessness, loss of contact with biological parents, physical abuse in the family, early familiarity with the youth courts and the criminal justice system, a period in care are also underlined as common background problems.

I could not apply any of these criteria to Conor. He lost his father — my brother James died from cancer — when he was 21: a desperately sad family bereavement, but occurring too late in Conor's case to have been "an early experience". Marie-Louise, his sister, in the memorial piece that she wrote, could think of nothing in their collective childhood which indicated the text-book background of the drug-addict. "We were a wholly normal, a fabulous family. We had the most easy-going father. We never wanted for anything. We had a mother who used to try and chase us around the kitchen every now and then with a wooden spoon. She'd never catch us, though. My parents had a very happy marriage." This I know to be true. Marie-Louise still remembers her own childhood as an idyllic time.

I did learn later on that Conor did suffer from clinical depression, and that he sometimes used anti-depressants to combat this. How strange that I had always thought of him as a joking, cheerful person, and was quite unaware of his depressive episodes.

The funeral Mass took place, followed by the burial.

The funeral of a young person is always well attended, for there are many survivors, many contemporaries who will mourn. Conor's mother and sisters were shaking with misery, and PK seemed completely bewildered. My sister Ursula had come from the United States and was blind with tears. My brother Carlos was limp with shock. There were many young people, drained and waxy in their dark clothes, black being such a curious colour theme of youth dress codes.

A lonesome tune was played on a tin whistle, one of those Irish melodies which manage to be both mournful and merry at the same time. PK was expected to read part of the lesson, but broke down in the speaking of it, and was helped by a friend, Dave. Dave was accustomed to funerals. Though only in his thirties, he had attended nine funerals of young friends over the past couple of years. The pressure of heroin use among his peers in Dublin had driven him to America.

There were so many tears. Conor's friend, Stephen Mulcahy, spoke a eulogy, which was funny and truthful. Conor was a bohemian, Stephen said. He didn't always turn up when expected, and he often did unexpected things; he was a joker; he was reckless and wild. His friends loved him for the way he was, and would not have had him otherwise. So be it.

Later, at the wake which followed the burial, another of Conor's friends said a little drunkenly: "Conor lived and died as an existentialist. He chose his life. He chose to live his life doing everything he wanted to do." This was an attitude I was to encounter again and again: it is an accepted value now, among the young. You make your choices; you choose your life; it's nobody else's business but yours, and there is nothing that anyone else can do about your choices. Nobody else is responsible for them.

There is an aspect of this philosophy which is courageous and robust. It is at the opposite end of the philosophy which claims that we are all passive victims of "society", or circumstance. But there is a shoulder-shrugging indifference behind all this existentialism, too.

Conor may well have chosen his way of life, but if we could roll back the film, and he could have been warned that this choice was death by heroin, would he have chosen it? I think not. I think it never crossed his mind, either.

Conor had been uncharacteristically affected by the death of Princess Diana in 1997. He and Marie-Louise and a former girlfriend of his, Hilary, a girl he might once have married — if only he had done! — had talked together about the video sequence when Diana is seen going out through the revolving doors of the Ritz Hotel that night of her death. Did the thought ever occur to her that these were her last hours? No, it did not. Now Hilary and Marie-Louise asked the same question of Conor: as Conor entered through the door of the Central Hotel — nice place, well appointed, recently renovated, but perilously close to an area where heroin is traded — did he ever think that he would never go out again? No, he did not.

A choice means the information must be available to you to make that choice. If you do not know that the choice you are about to make is potentially fateful, can you be making an informed choice?

Around the grave, under the Dublin hills at Dean's Grange, the young people gathered, with scanty clothes on a biting December day, their faces raw as the priest intoned the necessary ritual words, "In sure and certain hope of the Resurrection ..." as the coffin was lowered into the earth. Conor was buried with his father, a reunion thirty-six years on from that day when James had brought his infant son home from the hospital with such elation. Life and death intertwined so inseparably. Another filmic scene, too. The tears of women flowed.

I learned afterwards — some time afterwards — that those who use heroin do not feel the cold. An underdressed individual on a cold Irish winter's day must be a heroin suspect. Among the many, many things I did not know.

There was so much I didn't know about this culture. And so much I didn't care to find out, or to bestir myself to uncover. Until these deaths, I was obstinately ignorant and under-informed, particularly for a journalist who should be aware of social problems. Particularly for someone who had clocked up eight years sobriety after a habit of twenty-five years hard drinking.

Conor's wake, when the mourners returned to his mother's house, was the usual Irish mixture of sadness and lamentation, interspersed with moments of joking and even laughter. I think people have such a sense of disbelief, with the sudden death of a young person, that they forget themselves, momentarily, and expect him to walk in the door at any moment.

His brother Patrick looked dazed, but he did not seem drugged. We talked. We expressed our appalled feelings, our shock at what had occurred. "Nothing will ever be the same," he said miserably. "Ever, ever."

Clichés are sometimes true.

I held him, and then I felt how thin he was, how slight he had become under his flimsy jacket. He was shattered and exhausted and I told him that now, he must live Conor's life for him. He must, I said, sort out his own life, and remake it from the start. "Yes," he said, absently. "I must do something now to make Mammy proud of me."

Yet how wrong, stupid and naïve I was in delivering this lecturette. Others, including some of PK's friends, made the same mistake, saying that if there was one good thing that might come out of this dark night, maybe it would be the saving of Patrick. Maybe now, PK would be motivated to pull himself together, and quit the drug habit. What fools we all were. What insensitive, naïve, ignorant, under-educated, ill-informed and complacent *bien-pensants*. A committed heroin addict does not, cannot "pull himself together". A heroin addict has spent his choices. "You don't decide to be an addict," wrote William Burroughs in his classic testimony, *Junky*. "One morning you wake up sick and you're an addict."

You may decide to try heroin. Afterwards, it is the heroin that decides what happens. It is true, as I have since found out, that not everyone who has tried heroin, or who has used it occasionally, has become an addict. But about a quarter of people who use heroin will go on to addiction; because dependency to morphine sets in very quickly. As the medical profession — which is so sparing in administering it even in mortal pain — understands.

Conor's death was unusual — even a "freak accident" — because he was not seen by any of his friends as an addict. He was just this recreational user. One of his friends, a successful businessman in his thirties said to me: "We all do drugs, Mary. Conor was just unlucky." It is accepted by some "recreational" users that some people will take heroin to come down from ecstasy.

But his younger brother was addicted, and was really powerless where the drug was concerned. PK needed an open discussion about heroin — not admonitory, supportive but not enabling — in which recovery was emphasised. The vague conversation we had about "getting your life together" was a useless piece of evasion on my part.

Thinking back on that conversation, I realise that Patrick had sought me out; and since his death I have found so many little messages from him among various letters and papers. He always kept in touch. He wrote thoughtful little cards, choosing pictures he knew I would like. He would give me books to suit my interests. I have a book he gave me, next to my bed, on "Celtic Spirituality". He put some thought into choosing that book, and wrote inside it, and I can hardly bear to read, now, the loving inscription.

He would come around to hang pictures for me. I was agreeable to him, but I think I didn't really want to be involved in his problems. I didn't extend enough of a helping hand. I too was an existentialist: "it's his choice".

Far from Conor's death being an opportunity to motivate PK to get clean, as some of us imagined, it had quite the opposite effect. It drove him further into the hopeless spiral of drug dependency. I now know that it is at the moment of grief and loss that heroin addicts need to be most especially monitored.

Even as Conor was being buried, even while his friends and peers were mourning him, heroin reigned and ruled. At that very wake, some of the mourners had their gear.

The days that followed Conor's death were bleak. It was the run-up to Christmas, but celebrations seemed inept. And dreary. A week after Conor's death, I spoke to his mother on the telephone. She hadn't been able to pray at first, but now she was doing so again. "I hope Our Lady will help me." His beautiful sisters, Marie-Louise and Sarah, were utterly bereft. The bleakness of it all.

Yet, there is anger after a death, as well as grief and denial. You wanted to go out and shoot the drug-dealers yourself. "Frankly," I said to someone, "I don't mind if the IRA does break the legs of heroin dealers. They deserve much worse." I also felt the police were complacent. Is heroin against the law or not? If it is, the constabulary should uphold the law. It is not their business to make "social" decisions, according to how they feel.

If the law was being implemented properly, then those who trade and use heroin should be busted. But the trade is carried on, I fulminated, quite openly. I saw things simply, in black and white, because I knew so little. I didn't appreciate then, as I came to see, later, that dealer and user are inextricably mixed. Most heroin users are, or have also been, dealers. How else do they get the money to fund the habit — besides, of course, stealing and shoplifting, which heroin users do routinely? Young women also resort to prostitution, since there is always a demand and supply in this trade too.

It is also possible that the two brothers shared heroin sources, which must have been a terrible source of remorse to the grieving Patrick, and a bitter enlargement of his suffering. Although there was also evidence that Patrick had tried to discourage his brother from using, letters he had written, though never sent.

As Christmas came nearer, I went to gatherings at friends' houses, and heard so many accounts of young people who use heroin. Beautiful young girls with AIDS.

Beautiful young girls, pregnant, with HIV. Sons who had struggled for years with the drug problem. Young men who had seemed to have everything to live for, caught in the heroin web. Young people with lifelong hepatitis. Everyone knew some family with the affliction. It struck me then, again, how much the problem affects a whole family, and friends too. This existentialist — "it's his personal choice" — did not accord with the fact that if the choice is individual, the impact is collective.

I could hardly face my sister-in-law, seeing the grief which assailed her: all Conor's possessions were around, his room stuffed with film, books, notes, cards, archives of every kind.

Yet we went about our business unaware of the unfolding tragedy, heedless of what was to occur.

When something awful happens, every moment of that day is freeze-framed for all eternity, it seems, in your memory. Every minute logged, every detail fixed in the video of the conscious mind. And always the futile wish: if only we could rewind the tape, go back and intervene before the tragedy strikes. This time-machine dream stayed with me for months and months: every time I saw a newspaper pre-dating the tragedies, every time I had do my tax accounts, or look up any retrospective archive. "That was Before." If only one could go back.

I can see every frame of that fatal Christmas Eve. The search for a taxi to meet three friends for breakfast. The exact number of coins I paid the cabbie, when I found one. The traffic jams around Stephen's Green because of a public party for Gay Byrne, the broadcaster. Then, the lunchtime journey out to Glenageary, beyond Dun Laoghaire, by the Dart train: the bay of Dublin looked clear and lovely that day. The conversation I overheard between two youths on the train, discussing their experiences of working in England and Ireland. "It's so much better here, now, in every way," said one, as we passed the sea at Blackrock.

Alighting, I said to my husband — "We can't stay too long. There's still last-minute shopping to do." Every aspect of that Christmas Eve lunch is a movie constantly replayed in my head: the pâté, the fishpie, the delicious gooseberry tart, the merry bantering over the meal. Every banal thing is imprinted, and when the memory retrieves it, the caption says: "At this moment it was still not too late. At that moment it was still not too late."

As the shops closed around 5.30, and my son Edward and I loaded up the car in Merrion Square, there was a brilliant winter sunset, a crimson sun in an electric blue sky. At 17.30, it was still not too late.

At around that time, PK was going for a drink in Grogan's pub, just behind Grafton Street in Dublin. After Conor's death, he did, as a matter of a fact, make an effort to conquer heroin, and to start on a course of methadone, a replacement legal drug used to maintain heroin addicts and wean them off the greater evil. But maybe Christmas is not a good time to start new habits or chuck old ones. Especially a Christmas of grief.

I say that my younger nephew died of heroin, but that isn't the whole truth. Clinically, PK actually died of a cocktail of methadone, heroin and alcohol, known as a polydrug death. He had, according to a close friend, taken 40 milligrams of methadone — as medically prescribed — on the morning of his death. He had done his Christmas shopping, and left the gifts, wrapped up, at her mews flat (where he also left the bottle of methadone). He saw some friends at the pub that evening. He had a drink with my son Patrick, his cousin, and they had had a nice time together. The cousins were good companions, and PK had generously helped my son with some historical research. Pat West had said to PK: "I will be your brother now."

And the last words my son Patrick said to his cousin were "See you tomorrow", and PK had replied he was looking forward to that. He was to join us for lunch in my Dublin flat on Christmas Day.

When PK didn't turn up at lunchtime, nobody was, initially, concerned. He could be late. It pains me to say I was even initially relieved. I loved him, but he was a worry. The heroin problem was an embarrassment, especially in the presence of my elderly uncle who was also coming to the Christmas meal. Uncle Jim, who has also since died, was a kindly but in some ways exacting man. You feel nervous putting on a family meal anyhow, and I'd rather see PK later, less formally.

Christmas Day itself is less imprinted on my mind now, because by the time it dawned, it was too late. It was too late to roll back the video. PK died before midnight. He had gone back to his bedsit, alone, perhaps meaning to join friends later, and had taken one last shot. It sent him into an everlasting sleep.

At about four-thirty in the afternoon, my elderly uncle had had enough and wanted to return to his own home, in Sandymount. I undertoook to drive him home, leaving behind my husband, two sons, my brother Carlos and his wife Louise, May, Marie-Louise and Sarah. I duly left Uncle Jim home and then returned to the flat, which is in the centre of Dublin. As I came in I heard my niece Sarah speaking on her mobile phone, and there was something terrible about her expression. "Patrick Kenny is dead," she cried. It was unspeakable, unrealisable. It was a scene from a J.M. Synge tragedy, when all the men have been taken by the sea: a strange and eerie wail went up from the two sisters that their second brother was dead. From the mother, a catatonic stillness. Sarah said the words, again — "Patrick is dead" — and I wanted to run away and hide from what had to follow.

Marie-Louise and Sarah, my son Patrick and I went to identify the body, driving in the silent Christmas evening streets, to the South Circular Road, an area where drug problems abound. We knew the house by the Garda cars parked outside. PK had just moved into this little flat a few weeks previously. It had been thought a good sign, a sign of progress, a sign that he was getting his life together, that he felt ready to move into a flat on his own. We ascended the stairs where his friends had broken in. And there was Patrick, in a kneeling, semi-foetal position, as he had keeled forward, taking the hit. His face was hidden but his beautiful black hair looked so healthy, still. He still wore his shoes.

There was a guard there already. An emergency doctor had been summoned, bearing the disgruntled look of a man who had not yet had his Christmas dinner. He proclaimed death by opiate overdose.

"Don't you ever enforce the law?" I said to the young policeman. "Drugs are against the law, you know."

"Drugs are a social problem," the policeman said, reiterating his sociological course from the police academy.

"Burglary is a social problem, but you don't passively allow it to go on."

"You're upset, Madam."

I found this patronising — his police academy sociologist had taught him that some old biddy would make irrelevant accusations in distress — and yes, I was upset, and angry. Angry that criminals facilitate the taking of young lives in this way. Angry that doctors apparently hand out bottles of methadone without, for all I knew, explaining that this is as dangerous a drug as heroin, and that statistically it kills more people than heroin. Angry with myself for not being more pro-active: this was when the self-anger, the repining really began.

And so, the wretched funerary drama had to be enacted once again. The funeral parlour where he lay, while we said a decade of the Rosary over the still effigy of this sweet young man. The funeral Mass, the readings, the spoken appreciations, the burial. And the weeping, weeping, weeping, of forlorn women, and the pale, white faces of young friends. Oh, Patrick, what a sword of sorrow pierced our hearts at your passing.

Never did the words, from the prayer my mother so loved — "Hail Holy Queen" — seem to apt. "To thee do we send up our sighs, mourning and weeping in this valley of tears: O clement, O loving, O sweet Virgin Mary." How deep is the need for human consolation from the spiritual springs of the divine.

PK left so little behind him. His father's pen. Toy cars, his childhood playthings. Tapes — one marked "Patrick's Birthday". A prayer book and holy pictures, given by his grandmother, my mother, who he loved. A coffee pot — single tasse. Sunglasses. J.G. Ballard's novel "Cocaine Nights", which he was reading. A book I had given him from Alcoholics Anonymous: "Twelve Steps and Twelve Traditions." An address book. Social services card. A

"Dogtown Productions" card — that had been Conor's film company — with references to a film scenario, macabrely and presciently called "The End". A note from the girl to whom he had been married, in his early twenties, in the United States: "Pat... I miss your beautiful face." And his appended coda: "God, I love this girl more than anything."

Some fragments of writing, which indicated some of the pain and misery that heroin had brought him. "The subway doors open and you step into the speeding capsule and off you go on your sullen way to hell." Perhaps Patrick had wanted to be a writer: that was another conversation I never had with him.

If the older brother's death was a terrible accident, the younger's began to take on the shape and form of a tragic inevitability. I began to see, in retrospect, how his life had been going downhill. I had such a strong feeling that I had failed him. I failed to do what older people should do for younger people: advise: protect: lead: direct. Take an interest, for heaven's sake.

He wanted to please. He needed help, and I shrugged my shoulders, absorbed in my own life. Yes, I had given him the AA book, and I had once written to him, quite sternly. But I should have done much, much more.

The winter months stretched ahead, the cold hoar of frost on the ground as I drove in England and Ireland, mirroring the frozen feeling of exile that I had in my heart. The world seemed full of meaningless prattle and drivel. I had to find out about heroin. Why do people take it? What genie is in this bottle which beckons intelligent young people to their deaths? Why is it suddenly available in every city, in country towns, in villages — along with so many other drugs? And can these young lives be saved?

Why, I asked the passing landscape, Why?

Letter from Paul

I come from a good background and went to good schools and had a very loving family. But despite everything I had going for me I chose heroin. I must say that you do choose to be an addict, you are not a victim of a disease as some would say. Though the longer involved you are the more it feels like the drug comes looking for you. I have attended day centres around Dublin for around three years, and spent a year in Residential in County Laois. I have been on drugs since eleven years of age and using heroin since sixteen. I am now twenty-four. My drug habit went unchecked until I was about nineteen. I managed this because I do not, or at least not until this year fit the junkie photofit. I am well dressed and have been in the same job for three years. I have a three-year-old son whom I look after and I pay my bills.

Of late, though I have let things slide a bit, but I will kick the habit. I just hope that in your book you talk about the reality of what heroin can do to somebody. There have been times when I have wanted to o.d. but didn't want to be clean. I couldn't see life without heroin but I was finding life with it too much of a struggle. Six of my lifelong friends died over the last two years. My nineteen-year-old brother is also an addict. I hope that your book will educate those that need the education — the parents of now and the future.

All the best — Paul

Chapter Two

How Did We Get Here?
How the Heroin Culture Developed

Sex 'n drugs 'n rock 'n roll. That was what the 1960s were supposed to be about.
>   —James Kay and Julian Cohen: *The Parents Complete Guide to Young People and Drugs*, 1998.

Number of heroin users in Britain 1959: about 50
Number of heroin users in Britain 1990s: an estimated 250,000
>   —Ruggerio, et al: European Statistics: Elizabeth Young: *The Guardian*, 20 August 1994.

I knew nothing about the drug culture, in the 1990s. This was also a phrase I was to hear many times from parents and families of drug users: "We knew nothing about heroin. We were totally unaware of how widespread the drug culture is." Yet I was an experienced journalist who had been an active participant in the 1960s "cultural revolution", which is now acknowledged as the source, and the beginning of the end-of-century obsession with drugs. In going back to that source, in the 1960s, I even came across references to myself as being instrumental in helping the counterculture along through my role of youthful reportage.

Yet, back in the 1960s, I actually saw and experienced very little drug use. This was partly because it was much less ubiquitous; and partly because it was an aspect of the 1960s which didn't particularly interest me. Yes, I was drawn to the general idea of rebellion against the established order. But I became more attracted to the political side, and less drawn to the Sixties drugs and rock 'n' roll scene. My own drug of choice was alcohol; experiments with marijuana simply bored me.

Obviously, I tried it — I was a heavy smoker of Gitanes *sans filtre*, anyhow — but I had no sympathy or inclination for the hash effect. I thought dope smokers were silly and tedious, and I still think that tedium is the main impact it has on people. I don't disagree with the proposal that legalisation of cannabis should be considered and debated, but I cannot respect chronic marijuana smokers. Alcohol may make individuals aggressive, maudlin or inappropriately amorous, but at least, I would have argued, in its initial stage, it is often accompanied by witty conversation and hilarious stories.

Moreover, marijuana was so anti-work, so anti-achievement. It interfered with ambition. It interfered with my Becky Sharp agenda, which consisted of advancing my own interest through artful social manoeuvring. It interfered with going to five different parties in a night and meeting five different sets of people. It interfered with flying to Paris for lunch, which I thought a smart thing to do with a celebrity boyfriend of the time.

My alienation from the drug drug culture (as opposed to the alcohol drug culture) was established early, and I took little interest in the gradual spread of experimentation with various mind-altering substances. A crucial aspect of this was that I was not much interested in rock 'n' roll music: pop and rock — one turned into the other in 1967, it is said — was the secret key to drug culture. In contrast, I had odd, archaic musical tastes — I liked French music-hall (Piaf, Mistinguette, Charles Trenet), Fred Astaire singing "Let's Call the Whole Thing Off" and Ella Fitzgerald's incomparable performance of "Begin the Beguine". The Rolling Stones — two of whose hits were regarded by the American authorities as encoded messages about opiates ("19th Nervous Breakdown" and "Let's Spend the Night Together") — did nothing much for me.

I feigned being a Beatles fan for a while because I thought it irritated older people, which it did; but in fact I had a poster of Harold Wilson — the Labour Prime Minister in 1964 — on the wall where my flatmates had George Harrison or Donovan. I am so ignorant of these rock personalities that I actually did a television programme with Donovan in 1999 without knowing, even still, who he was. Well, we all have different hobbies, and the world of pop and rock was not my medium.

Throughout the Sixties, fully experienced in other respects in the "Swinging London" of the time, I only ever met one heroin addict. He was a friend of friends: he was called Tony and he used to come around very occasionally to a flat I shared in Bloomsbury with Miriam Doggart and a guy called Michael Jones. Tony wore dark glasses in the daytime and sat on our floor smoking and staring into space behind the dark bins. William Burroughs — a great cult writer for heroin users — describes the typical mood of the heroin user in *Naked Lunch* thus: "I did absolutely nothing. I could look at the end of my shoe for eight hours. I was only roused to action when the hourglass of junk ran out." And so it seemed, with Tony. When he came to visit us, he sat in a corner of the room doing nothing. He seemed harmless, but you weren't sure if he was there, or all there, at all. He was an object of curiosity, and concern, to other friends who wandered in and out. Now that I think of it, perhaps there was an element of fascinated glamour, too, as though he were a specimen from an unusual human zoo.

We knew that Tony had a Cinderella deadline every night: up until 1968, heroin addicts could be placed on a medical register in Britain (not in Ireland, where heroin has never been legally or medically available) and at midnight, London addicts would congregate at Boots the Chemist in Piccadilly, to pick up their next day's script. Poor Tony. It seemed an altogether wretched life, like being some kind of an invalid. As he would be waiting to go to Piccadilly to fetch what I saw as his squalid prescription, I might be taxi-ing off to the Dorchester or the American Bar at the Savoy to have a gorgeous cocktail with some movie director I was allegedly interviewing. Compare a Sidecar, a White Lady or a Between the Sheets with some ghastly pharmaceutical prescription that you stick in your arm? No contest. At that time, I was in no danger whatsoever of trying heroin, though had it been more normalised, more widespread, more easily passed around between peers, as it is today, then I surely would have been a candidate. And particularly if it had been available during the vulnerable adolescent years.

Thirty years on, I sought out Tony again. He had recovered in his thirties, after getting married and having a child — a not unusual pattern, I was to discover. He looked at his little daughter one day and thought — "I'm responsible for this life." He had built up a family business, and turned out to be a very pleasant guy: but a decade of his life had trickled through the hourglass, just looking at his shoe, waiting for the next fix.

Despite my indifference to the drugs and rock 'n' roll scene, I was aware of the "alternative" culture of the mid-60s, and even knew some of the counterculture pioneers: Richard Neville, (whose philosophy of "Playpower" had a very significant influence on London via *Oz* magazine) was a mate, and always an entertaining companion. I saw a fair bit of Jim Haynes, the American "alternative" entrepreneur who seemed to invent fringe theatre and brought the "happening" to Swinging London. I reported on Yoko Ono's first exhibition of "conceptual art", which I took for a spoof. But while I certainly knew that the times they were a-changing, I thought that the change would bring a political revolution, rather than merely a revolution in style and values which would leave democratic capitalism untouched.

Sure, I knew people took LSD trips — wasn't The Beatles "Lucy In The Sky With Diamonds" a signifier? — but after Jonathan Aitken told me that he had been visited by the most horrible visions of rivers of blood during an experiment with acid, I determined ever more firmly to stick to Margueritas, Kir Royales and bourbon on the rocks. Why blow your mind when you could lighten your heart with the cup that cheers?

And the drug culture in the mid-1960s was marginal, in an elitist sense. It was not a mass culture. Paul McCartney might do LSD, as he confessed in a magazine interview in 1967, but the average City secretary did not. Bob Dylan might write "Mr Tambourine Man" as an elegy to a drug experience, but not a lot of people knew that at the time. Drugs could be associated with pop stars, but usually disastrously, such as in the death of Brian Jones, of the Rolling Stones, who perished in a swimming pool as a very likely consequence of drug abuse. Brian Jones would apparently wake in the morning, take speed, cocaine, morphine, acid and Mandrax (a British brand of methaqualone, a pharmaceutical sleeping drug).

A famous police raid on the Rolling Stones in 1967 made sensational news, not least because Marianne Faithfull was found wearing only a sheepskin rug, but all this was about the bizarre life of celebrities, not about mainstream society. In 1999, by the way, Marianne Faithfull said: "If I could change anything in my life, it's that. I wouldn't bother with heroin. I really think it's a bit of a dead end. A bit of a mistake."

It is widely agreed among social historians that in the year 1968, western society underwent a radical shift: the big social changes that we have seen in the last quarter of the twentieth century are frequently dated from the events of that year. Some call 1968 the year of "the Gentle Revolution". More critically, Francis Fukyama has characterised it as the source of "The Great Disruption", of order, authority and family cohesion.

1968 was the year of student riots in America and the *evenements* in the streeets of Paris, of civil rights marches in Northern Ireland, of abortion legalisation in Britain — which was seen as a marker for women's freedom and autonomy — and the Prague Spring in Czechoslovakia which sowed the seeds of Soviet Communism's demise. The drug culture had not yet taken hold by 1968, but society was becoming more open to the values in which drugs like heroin would become acceptable. The catchphrase "If it feels good, do it" was fashioned for drugs. The musical *Hair* was the sensation of the year: the show's hit "Walking in Space" was interpreted, though only by the cognoscenti, as an allusion to drug experience.

In another strange twist of the narrative, by 1999, Marsha Hunt, who was the musical's star, was publishing a book in Dublin about the miserable and often hopeless lives of heroin addicts in Mountjoy prison. What was so very glamourous among rock celebrities in the 1960s had become, by the 1990s, the death sentence, or the purgatory of squalor, of some of the poorest and most disadvantaged.

What begins with elites spreads to mass culture within ten or fifteen years. Difficulties that elites can sustain, cushioned by wealth and social advantage, become much more disastrous for those down the scale. When the rich divorce, they divide their assets and hire more nannies for the children. When a poor family is broken up, it's down another notch on the poverty scale. The rich, like John Paul Getty, can recall, as he does in a new book by Harriet Vyner, that "we were all out of our minds on various substances". Fifteen years later, in various poor areas of inner cities, they were out of their minds on substances, too, with infinitely fewer resources to cope.

Drugs began to fan out over Europe during the 1970s. "During the late 1960s and early 1970s," notes a standard sociological history by Ruggerio, "there was evidence of increased use in some of the more northern European countries, including Britain, the Netherlands, Germany, Denmark and France. However, it was not until the second half of the 1970s that the supply and use of heroin escalated rapidly across Europe, including countries such as Italy, Greece, Switzerland, Austria and Greece, that had little prior experience of illicit heroin." Indeed, Ireland had virtually no abuse of dangerous drugs before 1978 — not even much cannabis — and had no appropriate legislation to control dangerous drugs before the Misuse of Drugs Act in 1977. Britain and Ireland were very different in this respect: between 1926 and 1968, there had been this medicalised tolerance of heroin use in the United Kingdom. Heroin has no history of medicalised prescription in the Republic of Ireland.

The "British system" had been quite admired for its typical British compromise (and, possibly, typical British hypocrisy, which can be another kind of compromise between ideal and reality). Doctors were permitted to prescribe heroin to addicts, if it was their honest medical opinion that the addict could not function otherwise, and could not control or halt the habit. This system seemed to work in quiet times, such as the 1950s, when heroin addiction was actually falling.

It was known, or suspected, that a handful of doctors were either over-sympathetic to the addicts, or in some cases amenable to remuneration by richer addicts. A colourful example of a liberal doctor was the late Lady Frankau, who had a London practice specialising in treating addiction. The picture of the Jewish mother, Isabella Frankau is said to have genuinely cared for her patients, among whom was the outstanding American jazz trumpet player, Chet Baker, for whom she prescribed heroin in 1962. (He died, ravaged by the drug, in 1988.) Dr Frankau had seen nothing wrong with helping him when he needed a prescription, and he came to London specifically to obtain the opiate.

Throughout the early and middle 1960s there was a continuous increase in the prescription of heroin, although it still only touched a tiny percentage of the population. Between 1961 and 1968, the number of heroin addicts notified to the Home Office rose from about fifty a year to one thousand a year. But as the use of heroin began to spread, this tolerant British system was increasingly abused, and medically prescribed heroin began to leak into the grey market: addicts would sell some of their legal heroin on to street users. Some doctors were clearly over-prescribing. In 1967, the regulation was radically altered, after which only specific psychiatrists working in rehabilitation clinics could issue such prescriptions.

By 1968, too, a new sort of heroin user was observed. In the 1930s and 40s, heroin addicts were often middle-aged folk who had become dependent on morphine for pain control. In the 1950s there were war survivors, and always some jazz musicians. In 1968, it was noted that a new generation of heroin users came from "the new youth cultures and bohemias of music and art". A steady trickle of Americans and Canadians were travelling to Britain to accommodate their heroin habit. Where one society seems more liberal than another towards the procurement of a given drug, there will be drug tourism.

During the 1970s, the use of other drugs was also spreading, not least pharmacologically prescribed drugs such as barbiturates and tranquillisers, referred to casually as "moggies and vallies" (Mogadon was a sleeping sedative, Valium a common tranquilliser). The medical profession was often irresponsible and promiscuous in these prescribing practices, and depressed housewives, troubled teenagers or women undergoing hormonal changes from the menopause would routinely come away from their doctor with a handful of tranqs. One of the Irish addicts that I spoke to in 1999 had been put onto a regime of tranquillizers, by a distinguished Dublin psychiatrist, in the mid-1970s — because she had been a "difficult" child. Her parents' decision to take her to a shrink for problem behaviour was regarded as highly enlightened, and a departure from the old authoritarian style of mere punishment for badly behaved kids. But starting on tranquillizers at eleven is a straight prescription for later addictive behaviour.

My own mother became addicted to Valium, in the 1970s, initially for the control of asthmatic attacks linked to the disease emphysema (which she had developed from cigarette smoking). Later she used Valium to cope with grief and depression, of which she had her share in her last years. Though she wasn't to know, I believe the example of seeing Valium routinely used in the household was to have a long-term deleterious effect on my nephews; my own increasingly uncontrolled drinking wasn't much of an example either.

Attitudes to drink were also becoming more liberal over this period. The last echoes of Victorian temperance traditions were disappearing, and in both Britain and Ireland, it became ever more socially acceptable for women, and for younger people, to drink openly. Formerly, there had been social taboos associated with drunken women — which naturally we younger feminists challenged: competitive cries to the effect of "I can drink any man under the table" issued from our lips. Older women encouraged us: they looked back with anger at the way in which women had been excluded from the social life of pubs, or only barely allowed into the snug, in times gone by.

And the freedom to drink began to move down the age scale generally. Among my elder sister's generation, the first glass of sherry was traditionally taken at a twenty-first birthday party. Among mine, it was acceptable to drink a little something alcoholic at eighteen or nineteen. Soon it would be fifteen or sixteen. We thought this excellent. We were becoming more European, more civilised about drinking openly.

While the drug culture, in its many manifestations, was spreading during the 1970s, I have no recollection of being particularly conscious of it at the time. I knew that some people took illegal drugs, just as I knew some people were involved with prostitution; but it all seemed a faraway underworld which didn't touch me, my friends, my family or the civil society around me. I had married and had two sons, and the delightful years of caring for young children absorbed me. My husband, Richard West, had reported from Vietnam in the 1960s and 70s, and had written three books about Vietnam: he knew how the American and Australian soldiers had become involved with both cannabis and heroin during the terrible war there. He regarded the role of drugs as a symbol of American decadence; the cruelties of that war were enforced via mind-altering substances. He pointed out that the word "hashish" was derivative from "assassin". He had few illusions that the "flower power" culture would lead to more "peace and love". The shocking murders carried out by Charles Manson apparently under the influence of drugs, in 1969, had quenched many hippy dreams.

The American involvement in Vietnam had boosted the drug trade in South-East Asia. The so-called "Golden Triangle" where the borders of Laos, Burma (now called Myanmar), Thailand and the south-west tip of China meet was the main source of supply for Western heroin addicts.

It is claimed that the American intelligence service, the CIA, encouraged, or even created, this trade. Because the CIA required the assistance, during the Vietnam war, of highland tribesmen near North Vietnam who grew opium as a cash crop, this opium farming was bolstered. (Heroin is derived from opium — it was first synthesised by a British scientist in 1874, just twenty-one years after Alexander Wood helpfully invented the hypodermic syringe in the United States.) The American authorities clearly were concerned by the problems associated with heroin by the early 1970s: Congress and the Senate began passing legislation introducing methadone maintenance programmes for heroin addicts in 1971 and 1972.

The heroin in common use during this decade was known in street parlance as "Chinese white". It came from the Golden Triangle, was taken by injection, and the end product was not initially high in heroin content. In 1980, the average bag of street heroin in the U.S. was four per cent pure; by 1998, it was around seventy-one per cent pure. And it was different heroin.

In 1979, two events occurred which were to change the course of heroin addiction, making the substance more accessible, cheaper and easier to take. The Shah of Iran was deposed. And the Americans moved to support the rebels of Afghanistan who were fighting against the Soviet Union.

The Shah's regime was reactionary, but it had more or less kept in check the huge capacity for opium production in Iran, historically known as Persia. In 1955, the Shah had imposed a ban on domestic opium production, though some legal production was permitted to supply registered addicts. Towards the end of the 1970s, the Shah's dictatorial hold grew weaker, and opium farmers increasingly ignored the ban. When the

Shah fell, the turbulence of the Iranian revolution brought a window of opportunity to opium traffickers. And then the rich Iranian exiles left Teheran with the one dowry which could earn them revenue in the West: suitcases full of brown heroin.

In the same year, the CIA was apparently willing to "look the other way" as the Afghan rebels traded opium for guns. Within the space of a year, Afghanistan was supplying more than sixty per cent of the American heroin "market".

In the summer of 1999, I drove to a pretty farmhouse in Sussex to talk to Clarissa, a forty-year-old mother now settled into country life with her young children: she explained exactly what the impact of "Golden Brown" — the Iranian heroin — had on the London scene in the early 1980s. She had been a young art student from a gifted but much-married family of the arty upper class. Chelsea, she recalled, was suddenly awash with Iranian brown. It was cheap. It was everywhere. And, most important of all, you could smoke it. You had to inject Chinese white, but Iranian brown was just so much easier to use. The majority of people are not attracted to the idea of introducing needles and syringes into their veins, as a social experiment: but smoking (or snorting) made it much, much more accessible. Those who smoked heroin might afterwards progress to injecting — after dependency had set in.

Smoking heroin was not so different from smoking hash, and not so very different from smoking a cigarette (over ninety per cent of heroin users are also cigarette smokers). To smoke heroin, you didn't need the complicated array of "works" (syringes, acid, tourniquets), and if it made you a little ill at first — nausea is a usual response to the first hit — it soon made everything seem all right with the world. For Clarissa, it helped her overcome her sense of anxiety, her youthful lack of confidence, her fear of competition, her feelings of inadequacy, fear of not being attractive enough, not having the right clothes, not being glamourous enough, not measuring up to the Julie Christie ideal of the time. Why a beautiful woman with promise, a kind personality, and a flat in Chelsea should be visited by these feelings of anxiety and inadequacy is puzzling to those without these advantages. But that is the way things are.

And as society became more liberated, in one sense, it also became more frightening, more competitive, more full of confusing choices and anxious expectations for young people. The generation of the 1950s had grown up in a world of tightly controlled norms; you might rebel against them, but you knew what was expected. Men, in many countries, did military service; women were repeatedly told by the magazines and the agony aunts that they were expected to go to the altar as virgins. University life was a web of rules and regulations: up until the late 1960s, Oxford and Cambridge colleges maintained draconian bans on the mixing of the sexes, and a fellow could be sent down if a girl was discovered in his rooms overnight. There were ways around this, but it entailed ingenuity and a conscious bending of the rules. By the 1980s, the norm of personal freedom and person autonomy was everywhere gaining ground, much to the benefit of those psychologically empowered to use their freedom and autonomy; but frightening, too, in the way that boundaries and limitations were so quickly dissolving.

The sex revolution had freed up individuals, and the horrors of an unwanted pregnancy receded — not just because of birth control, but also because being an unwed mother was losing its stigma. Yet new anxieties were taking the place of discarded ones. There was now a category known as "being good in bed". Did you measure up to this form of consumerist testing? Drugs were certainly a way of helping a worried young person to cope. The criminal fraternity was quick to perceive its own "window of opportunity", and throughout the 1980s crime cartels moved into heroin (and cocaine) distribution. As a European sociologist puts it: drugs had moved from the counterculture to the enterprise culture.

In Ireland, as elsewhere, organised crime was expanding, as it does in times of change, and prosperity. By the same token, the influence of the Catholic Church was beginning to wane, its moral grip on authority weakening, and, also significantly, its intensely experienced rituals and sacrilised rites being simplified, or even abandoned. In 1969, when Martin Cahill was twenty years of age, crime was rare in Ireland and the Garda Siochana could boast a crime detection rate of nearly a hundred per cent. Cahill, who was to become known as "The General" helped to change all that. His career is a fascinating reflection of the crime explosion over the next twenty years, during which time Cahill netted £40 million in the theft of art, jewels and cash. The Troubles in Northern Ireland were instrumental in criminalising the whole country, via guns and bank robberies. Cahill himself was personally opposed to drugs — his brother had died of heroin — and "wouldn't work with junkies": he even said that drugs damaged the criminal profession.

Yet the explosion in crime, and the explosion in drug trafficking, were all of a piece, since illegal drugs are trafficked via crime, and in turn produce addicts who turn to crime. Cahill's former crime partners, the Dunne family — Shamie, Mickey, Larry and Boyo — were the principal gangsters who introduced the first wave of heroin in Ireland, in 1980 and 1981. Tony Felloni, Dublin's "heroin boss" and "King Scum" — as vividly described in Paul Reynolds' biography — was another crucial agent in making heroin available. It started in the inner city neighbourhoods where a large youth population — half of Ireland's population was under twenty-five — and a state of chronic unemployment made for easy pickings. What went for the Kings Road in Chelsea went equally for the old slums of Sean O'Casey's Dublin.

All through the 1980s, the dance culture and "club culture" were making the use of ecstasy almost ubiquitous. Ecstasy, a chemical hallucinogen, began as a "designer drug" in New York in the late 1970s and reached Europe in the mid-eighties. Just as rock music was linked to amphetamines and cocaine, reggae with cannabis, ecstasy was the drug of the dance music scene. Users of ecstasy describe it as five times safer than paracetemol (about a million people in Britain are said to use it weekly) and that its "huggy-kissy" euphoric mood makes it a much nicer, much less aggressive drug than alcohol. But all drugs have side-effects, and ecstasy can bring flashbacks and depression. It may also lead the unwary on towards other drugs, including heroin. Heroin can "bring you down" comfortably after the excitations of ecstasy. And any mass use of drugs enhances the drug culture.

*

In 1983, my brother James had a recurrence of the cancer which had first touched him in 1976, and from which he seemed initially to have made a good recovery. In many families, there is a special family "star": the one who is the focus of all eyes, the magnetic centre of dynastic energy, the personality who seems to embody the whole family tradition. This was James. He was adored within the family, and outside of it too. Fifteen years after his death, I am still stopped in the streets of Dublin by strangers who once knew him, who ply me with stories of his gentleness, his humour, his marvellous conversation. He was an extraordinary, unforgettable character. He also had a quick-tempered, and frustrated, side to his personality; he came of a generation — those born in the 1930s — who got little opportunity to fulfil themselves creatively, to choose their careers, to carry on further education. His growing illness, from the autumn 1983, was a prolonged anguish. His death in July 1984 cast a shadow of great grief over his wife, daughters, sons, mother, sisters, brother. I remember looking at the bare, thorny trees over a steel-grey sky over our family home in Ballsbridge Dublin, in that December 1984 and feeling a wintry sense of the forlorn. That Christmas, the family seemed inconsolable.

The loss of an adored parent, the grief of death, the example of Valium use and a possible "drinking gene" in the family: plus a remedy flooding into Dublin which promised to wipe away all tears. This all came together in the mid-1980s. What I didn't know then — what none of us knew — was that this is the worst possible combination for any young person susceptible to the lure of heroin. I now see that it was virtually inevitable that my nephew Patrick, then a vulnerable fifteen, would be drawn first to softer drugs, and then to heroin. But it took me a long quest of learning about the drug culture, from users, families of users and those experienced in treatment to find that out. I embarked on an education in drugs rather late in the day.

The Heroin User — a Statistical User.

Average age of first trying an illegal drug: sixteen-and-a-half. Younger addicts start younger — fourteen-and-a-half.

Reasons for becoming dependent on drugs:

The need to get a buzz (39%)

The need to escape from problems (34%)

Boredom (31%)

Pressure from friends (25%)

Parents took drugs (7%).

How the habit is financed:

Shoplifting (48%)

Drug dealing (29%)

Fraud (29%)

Burglary (25%)

Other theft (19%)

Begging (12%)

Mugging (5%)

Summary of Psychological Well-Being of Drug Addicts.

Addicts are more bored, restless, depressed and unhappy with life than the general population.

They are a lot more lonely and remote, and their alienation can lead to suicidal thoughts. Just under a third (30%) admit to suicidal thoughts over the past three months.

Obstacles Faced When Addicts Sought Help

Lack of Community Treatment or Local Clinics

An unsympathetic GP

Lack of understanding in the community

Lack of practical support in employment or
  housing

Unable to admit their problem to friends or family

Fear of admitting their drug problem

Men tended to request more community support;
  women wanted more family support.

From: *Drugs: A Study Among UK Heroin Addicts*. May
1999, Gordon Heald of ORB, 9-13 Cursitor Street,
London EC 4A 1LL

Chapter Three

Not the Photofit Addict — Vicky's Story.

As I went in search of heroin users and their families, I discovered that a heroin addict can come from any kind of background. Poor people may be more numerous in the statistical picture; better-off families are simply better placed to seek help and private support. Even so, young people from all kinds of backgrounds can perish from heroin.

Vicky Remnant lives in a pretty little village in East Anglia. The 17th century farmhouse which is her home is enchanting, and there is a picture-book English garden. There are two over-enthusiastic dogs. The community is neighbourly and supportive. Vicky is a lovely person, a qualified nurse and a reflexologist. She has been married to Giles for twenty-five years, and there were two sons, Charles and Alistair. There is no history of alcoholism or other addictions in the family. They were a happy and united family: but their much cherished younger son became a heroin addict.

In Vicky's account of Alistair's schooldays were all the classic, tell-tale signs of a drug problem building up: a sensitive schoolboy who tried to please older peers, a decline in schoolwork, problems with money, and the onset of a continuing cannabis habit.

'We always hoped that the boys could talk to us about anything. We always said that — if you ever have problems of any kind, if you get a girl pregnant or anything, for goodness sake tell us, and we'll always be there, by your side.

He started into drugs when he went to his public school. He was dyslexic, which was a difficulty for him. Extremely bright. But he was very frustrated about putting things onto paper. His intelligence didn't come over well that way.

My eldest son Charles was at Harrow. But we chose to put Alistair into Stowe, [from age twelve] who were more helpful about this dyslexia problem. And we now know that he started using drugs in that first year. It was some time before anyone knew what was going on.

There was a Sixth Form of older boys who were using, and they used to get hold of the younger boys, and get them to bike to the nearest town and hand in the order to the newsagent. And apparently the drugs would arrive up at the school by taxi, and a certain older boy would take charge of them. This was mostly cannabis, and then LSD.

Alistair was great fun, with a great personality. He was six foot by the time he was twelve and I think the Sixth Formers found him very gullible. We had absolutely no idea what was going on, apart from the fact that he was frightfully keen that his bike was in good working order when he was going back to school. And I used to think, how lovely, he's taking all this exercise biking up there, as it's actually quite a way to go. The school allowed that, as it is very much out in the countryside. None of us realised what was going on. I don't think the school knew at that stage. This would have been about 1991.

Certainly when we talked to the headmaster, he said this school doesn't have problems with drugs. We were very ignorant about the long-term effects of drugs ourselves.

Alistair seemed to be very happy at Stowe, especially with his music. But in his last year, his work began to suffer. He wanted to leave and go to Sixth Form College in Cambridge. He had some very very nice friends. Absolutely delightful. We still keep in touch, and they are absolutely devastated. They also dabbled around the same route, but they have different personalities.

I had no idea that he was an addictive personality. All during his schooltime, I had no idea. He was huge fun to be with, very warm, kind, popular, an extrovert. He and his brother had a great friendship. Totally different but great friends. I always used to say how lucky I was that they were such good friends.

My husband was away a great deal, travelling. But we very much pulled together as a family. Charles was hard-working, studious and Alistair was a bit of a rogue. But they had a great rapport together. If anything, Charles used to turn to Alistair for advice. If he was planning to go on holiday, he'd say, "I just want to talk to Alistair about it."

He very much wanted to do his A levels at Cambridge, so that he could be at home. He felt he had had enough discipline at boarding school. And at that stage we had no inkling of what was going on. We felt that he was struggling with his work a bit. He got all his GCSEs. And yet he was not sure what he wanted to do with his life. Music had always been a very important part of his life.

He took his A levels with a view to doing pharmacology, believe it or not. So he did biology and sociology at A level to do pharmacology. The first year he lived in Cambridge with a family, nice family, a bit chaotic, but nice. The staff of the Sixth Form College seemed very sweet. But his work began to be not as good as it should have been, so he got a bit of extra help and tuition.

During that first year, I can't really say what the tell-tale signs were ... but by the end of that first year, he was not achieving as probably he should have been. We discussed it, we went to all the Sixth Form College parent evenings, and we were slightly concerned about this work side. But he was always a bit of a rebel and work was never his number one thing.

At the end of the first year, he was just seventeen. He said to us that he would rather come and live with us at home, because he had passed his driving test, and he would rather drive into college each day. We thought that would be rather nice. Then in the second year of A levels, the problems really started.

We realised that he had started not attending college. Money started to be a problem. He always seemed to need more money, which we first put down to books and things. He was doing a big art project and that seemed to need finances.

What had happened is that we had gone for our normal holiday to Cornwall, which we always did. We used to have barbecues on the beach. One morning I was picking up some clothes to put in the washing machine and I found a pipe among Alistair's clothes. I asked, what was this? He said it was a friend's, who had lent it to him. But he did admit that he might take the odd smoke of cannabis on the beach. I was about to throw it away and he said "Oh don't throw it away Mum, I can always sell it on to a friend." And we said we weren't happy about that at all, and we threw it over the edge of a cliff.

Unbeknown to us, he was absolutely addicted to cannabis by that time. We did not know at all, at that time.

In Cambridge, he had mixed with a very very bad lot of friends. What worried us was that we never met any of them. And by the Easter, when he was coming up to A levels, we were extremely concerned really. He had been missing a lot of school. He seemed erratic, unreliable. But he was very, very charming. He had a way with him.

At the time of A levels, he was actually in a terrible state. Giles, my husband, said to him, what is going on? we're here to help you ... We asked Charles what was going on, and Charles said, please Mum, don't get involved. He didn't want to be disloyal to Alistair either. And he felt it would sort itself out.

We then became very concerned. Giles heard from a friend of his that if you take a hair sample from the head, it can tell you what has been going in your life in the last six months. So unbeknownst to Alistair, we took some hairs from his pillow, had it sent off for analysis. And it showed us there and then he was on heroin, cocaine and cannabis.

He was then just eighteen. We sat him down and said to him, look Alistair, we know what is going on. He was absolutely devastated and broke down, and said, Oh Mum, I've been wanting to tell you everything. He was relieved that we knew. And then he said I think I can give it all up when the pressure of my A levels is over.

I had been talking to my senior partner at the medical practice, and she basically said, there is not a great deal you can do until it is out in the open. So I then told her what our findings were.

We then agreed that university was probably not right for him, because of his dyslexia. He under-achieved very badly at A levels. He managed to pass, but not particularly well. We agreed that he could go to a very good college in London to do technical music. It was a nine-month very intensive course, where you basically get a diploma to be a sound recording engineer, which is what he really wanted to do. We felt that he should do what he wanted to do. A gap year was out of the question, and he agreed. He was extremely keen on this. And we felt if that's what he really wants to do, then we must support that and help him.

So he went to the college in September. He lived in a flat in London with three other people who we had connections with, but didn't actually know. They were all very nice. Cromwell Gardens. Very nice flat.

To start with, things went well. But tragically, he went back down. He had said that he had given it all up. And there were no actual signs that he had gone back to it. But the moment he got to London — he went late September — we became pretty suspicious fairly early on that things were not right. He seemed to be always asking for money — little bits, you know, not large amounts. £20 and £30 here and there.

I used to go up to London sometimes — at that time I was doing my reflexology once a month. When I used to go up, he used to have supper with me, and always we used to notice that by ten o'clock in the evening, he always had to leave us. He always had to make an excuse and go — he was going to do music, or something. But tragically, he wasn't. He was going to join some heroin friends.

So in November, I went to Dorset with a friend. I spoke to him on the phone, and I said "I'm sure all is not well," and he said, "Mum, I'm coming home on Thursday." He came home on Thursday and absolutely collapsed on us. He said, "Mum, I'm right back to square one. And I'm at the stage of injecting." That was November 1996.

He cried his heart out, and he looked terrible. And one of the girls in the flat, a sweet girl — he had spent days withdrawn in the flat — she was only eighteen or nineteen, she said, you've got to tell your parents. That evening I sought help from the doctors in our practice, and he was straight on to methadone.

I was devastated, but I was so grateful that he was able to see the doctors. So he then went into the care of our GP, who put him straight on to methadone. Which made him feel very ill. I now wish he had gone straight into detox there and then. But at the time, it was felt that it was the right thing to do. Alistair was a patient of his, yet I was working there as a nurse. I was always very careful to keep in the background and not to intrude.

He was then sent for counselling to our local drugs counselling group. He liked his counsellor very much — a sweet woman who he saw on a regular basis. It was very helpful. Slowly, slowly they tried to reduce his methadone dose.

All during this time, he continued with cannabis. He was allowed to do that. It was felt that, anything to get him off the heroin. He was allowed to smoke it in his bedroom here. I would find myself in this extraordinary situation, where I would drive him up to Cambridge, I would park the car around the corner, and he would go and buy the cannabis and bring it back here. It was an extraordinary situation. I used to feel quite ill. But at that time, it actually was a help to him and the doctors believed it was best. I knew I was doing something totally against the law, and totally against my feelings — I have never had a drug in my life — but it's extraordinary what you will do for your child. But actually it was very mild compared to heroin, which is a killer.

That Christmas, we had already booked to go to Bali, all four of us, which we got through air miles. That was quite a difficult time. We had to get a dispensation to take methadone through Singapore, to Bali. We said to Alistair that on no account was he to take in cannabis. So we went to Bali. It was a difficult time, he felt very ill, not having cannabis: he didn't smoke, he didn't drink any alcohol. But we had as happy a family holiday as we could. And we had that lovely time together. Then we came back, and we had Alistair at home until Easter time, which was difficult for him, because he was very lonely being stuck out here, without any friends. He didn't do a great deal: gardened, walked. He was interested in cooking, he had a lot of musical equipment. We used to go up to Cambridge to see friends. But by the time we got to Easter, we needed to decide, what is he going to do?

He was such a lovely young person . The last person in the world you would imagine would have a problem. Of course, nobody knew at all, around here. They didn't need to know. So we agreed that it would probably be good if he could get back to London, get back into the course. He was very keen to do that. So we supported his decision.

He found a very nice flat — he wanted to be on his own. He was continuing with the counselling and the methadone. He came back to see our GP every weekend. He was then given weekly amounts of methadone to take back to London, which in retrospect might not have been wise. So he was, I think, misusing. And he told me afterwards that when he was back in London, he was back onto heroin.

He was back in college in Easter 1997, and the course would take him through to Christmas. All seemed to go well to start with. He stayed in London and completed the course at Christmas '97. And he didn't pass it. And he didn't get his diploma. Which was very sad for him.

We knew this in January and he relapsed again. The GP said to him: "Alistair, we have to get you into detox." We had to wait from January into May to get into a psychiatric hospital.

After that he was back home being counselled. He was counselled here and also once a week in Cambridge. He now got methadone on a daily basis. The GP was absolutely marvellous.

It was a difficult time, but we had a happy time. There were lonely times for him. But he was absolutely determined to go through with this detox. He wanted to get well. He wanted to go out and lecture to other people about drugs. He went in for his detox in May, where they take out all the opiates in your system. You have special nursing care. It went very well. We were not allowed to see him for several days. But it went very well.

He had such a lovely personality. There was a girl there who had suffered from post-natal depression and tried to commit suicide. Alistair was sweet to her, and used to spend hours with her.

People tend to think that if you are a heroin addict, you're a bad person. It's not true. But it takes you down that route of squalor. There is the terrible secretiveness.

We have been so lucky. Until the very last day of his life, he was never affected, really, by the drug. His personality remained a lovely personality, utterly charming, and kind. He was totally together. You would have no idea.

[Alistair was detoxed, but relapsed again. He was then admitted to the private clinic, The Priory, at Chelmsford, which costs £3,000 a week. He stayed there several weeks, and came out in good health, though he had never quit cannabis, even during his time at the rehab clinic. The after-care was a very difficult period for him. He was medically put on benzodiazopines, to help him cut down on cannabis, and he became addicted to these. He also drank. There was yet another relapse.]

We always gave him the support. He never exasperated us. My husband was wonderful to him. We never lost patience. There was trouble over money — he passed cheques that were forged. We were furious with the bank. The bank just said, "It's your son, it's your problem". They took no responsibility for not scrutinising the cheques.

Of course we would never have involved the police or the law. No. It may work for some people, but it wouldn't work for us. Alistair was too gentle a person.

He was home for about six or eight weeks, before he died, which was a lovely time, really. He enjoyed that time. We talked a lot. He was a very unusual character. He felt that there was a tremendous amount of suffering in this world. He had seen things in his twenty years that some people never see or feel. Somehow I knew that was a very special time, having him at home.

After all this, he thought he would have a total change of direction, in terms of careers. Perhaps the music world wasn't right for him. We went to a careers counsellor, a very nice man. That's when we decided that maybe he should aim for the motor industry. Fresh start. Not terribly academic, not terribly pressurised. But he was interested in cars. We used to have great laughs about it, great fun.

The last week, he was very unwell. He took a large concoction of drugs. Benzos, Valium, tranquillisers. I used to give him reflexology.

My husband had a friend in the motor industry, and Alistair left here that morning to go for an interview in London. Despite everything, he left our home, bright, sparkling, full of optimism. The interview went well and the chief executive said he was just the sort of young person they wanted. And yet tragically, after that ... came the end.

He had said to us that he wanted to stay down in London that evening, he wanted to see a few friends. He phoned about half-past-nine, and he said, "Mamma, I'm having such a lovely time, I'm so happy, I'm going to stay down. I'm absolutely fine." He was so happy. I said "Please come back tomorrow as Charles will be here." He said he would, but that he was absolutely fine. And I think that just before that conversation he had used.

He was just twenty-one. You can't lock them up.

That Saturday, he had got up in the morning, and you know, heroin users, they have a lot of baths. Baths are very very helpful — if you have a hot bath, it's very therapeutic, relaxing. Went into the bathroom. Tragically, the shot he took knocked him unconscious straight away. And he fell against the bathroom door, which blocked the door. By the time the friends realised that Alistair hadn't come out of the bathroom, they couldn't get the door open. They thought they could hear a snore, which was actually suffocation. And by the time the ambulance crew arrived and knocked the door down, he was pulseless.

They tried resuscitation and he was taken to Chelsea Hospital. He was pronounced dead at nine o'clock in the morning. He had got up about eight. He had used the heroin and it had knocked him unconscious.

I thank God he wasn't resuscitated, as he would have been on a life support machine. The amount of brain damage would have been awful. He didn't deserve that.

By lunchtime, we were very concerned that Alistair hadn't come home. We started to ring round some of the friends. Then Charles said, "Here's a police car coming up the lane." I knew immediately.

So we then went down to London. It was terrible for Charles. The hospital was wonderful. A young staff nurse, very upset, said "You'll have to identify your son". He looked very peaceful. It's an extraordinary thing to have to do. I'm a great believer in life after death and I felt he was at peace. But it was devastating. For everyone. His friends were devastated. Some of his friends from Cambridge, they were not a bad lot, but they were into the drug world.

I said to his friends who were into drugs, I am here for you all the time. Underneath, they're sweet people. Very sweet people.

They announced it in church that Sunday morning. We had the funeral on the Friday — the coroner's court released Alistair very quickly. Alistair was safely back with us on the Wednesday and we had the funeral on the Friday. The sun shone beautifully and he is buried under this beautiful young beech tree. We had all the music that he wanted — he told me he wanted the music from "The Mission". He used to listen to that music a lot. We had huge baskets of flowers by his grave — I wanted all the young people to feel part of this, to pay their last respects. Because some of them had been down that road with him. And then they all came back here afterwards. I was given an extraordinary amount of strength. Inner strength, and a huge amount of love. It still continues.

At his funeral the vicar talked about heroin addiction. And we have been very open since. A lot of people do not understand, unless they've been through it.

I thank God for Alistair's life.'

Mary Kenny

Lady Heroin — a Prisoner's Poem

(This anonymous poem has been passed around among prisoners in England.)

'Something Evil Comes This Way'
  – William Shakespeare

I will seduce you and make you my slave.
I've sent men stronger than you to their grave.
You think you could never become a disgrace,
And end up addicted to poppy seed waste,
So you'll start to inhale one afternoon,
Then you'll take me in your arms very soon,
And once I've entered deep down in your veins,
Your life will never be quite the same.
You'll need lots of money as you've been told,
For, darling, I'm much more expensive than gold.
You'll swindle your mother without thought or fear
You'll let your child starve if it gets you the gear
You'll mug and you'll steal for my venomous charm,
And feel true contentment when I'm in your arms.

The day when you know the monster you've grown,
You'll silently promise to leave me alone.
You think that you've got the mystical knack,
Well, sweetie, try getting me off your back.
The vomit, the cramp, your guts in a knot,
Your trembling nerves scream for just one more shot.
Hot sweats, the cold chills, the withdrawal pains
Can only be stopped by those little grains.
There's no other way, there's no need to look,
For deep down inside you'll know you are hooked
You'll give up your morals, your conscience and heart
And you will be mine until death us do part.

Chapter Four

What Kind of Person?
The Wellsprings of Addiction.

It's called heroin because you feel heroic. You feel better about yourself. That's where the name comes from.
  — Tom, fifty-two, lifetime addict.

FEEL GOOD
  — Poster advertisement for Lee Jeans.

Le Plaisir Avant Tout
  — French car advertisement.

What kind of a person becomes a heroin addict? Quite often, I would say, a very nice person. In my meetings with heroin addicts, it often struck me that these were among the most sensitive, intuitive and reflective individuals in our midst. They seem often to be people who feel the pain and suffering of humanity, and unable to bear what they feel, try to block it off. "Heroin," said Marek, an Anglo-Pole whose immigrant parents had come through hard times, "is a sane reaction to an insane world."

Heroin's ability to neutralise the emotions, to relieve feelings of isolation, and to make the user feel that he can manage life is underlined again and again. "It is the great comforter," says Alexander, a handsome-looking guy in his early thirties. "Whatever pain and rejection and embarrassment and guilt are in your life, heroin makes it better. You just don't have to deal with anything that's remotely painful."

"When you're on heroin," says another young man, Ben, who is in his twenties, "every insecurity, every self-doubt, guilt complex, every memory that shouldn't be there, everything that's ever, ever negatively affected you disappears. It's like floating in a warm bath of milk. It's like being back in the womb.

"Everything just disappears. Nothing matters. Noise, people, just blur. You just sit there and you're just so happy. I'd recommend it because it's the best high you'll ever have; but I wouldn't recommend it because it's the worst pain you'll ever feel."

The experiences of heroin are always remembered in a similar way, particularly in the early days of use. The warm bath, the removal of all emotional pain, embarrassment, guilt and rejection. To be sure, recovering addicts emphasise that this period only lasts a short time, and that once addiction sets in, the familiar pattern of dependency, secretiveness, marginalised living and crime is established. And boredom. "It becomes like being in some waiting room," says Alexander, who used heroin for twelve years. "Nothing happens. And then it's ten years down the road, and you've not moved on, you've just been wasting time. And that gets harder." That elusive first hit is pursued again and again, even when there are no veins left, and the old addict (if he survives) knows full well that he can never again experience that high. Some addicts actually get clean in order to start again from a base of restored health and yearning abstinence, just as some drunks get sober in order to have the thrill of a new drinking binge.

Much anti-heroin education emphasises the horrors of heroin — and quite correctly, for there are horrors indeed. Once dependency is established, the pleasure diminishes and heroin becomes more like a dose of insulin to the diabetic: something the body begins to crave just to stay in some state of normality. And heroin does screw you up, as a famous anti-heroin campaign once propagandised (it was shocking and it had no effect whatsoever, apparently). Yet it was descriptively quite true: your appearance deteriorates, your teeth rot, you become prematurely aged and your skin turns grey and mottled. Beautiful young women turn to scrawny hags within a few years on a diet of heroin. Their menstrual cycle may disappear, and dark hollows encircle their eyes. One of the long-time, "stabilised" heroin addicts I encountered was fifty: I could scarcely believe it. She looked seventy. The poor creature's teeth were black stumps.

But it is dishonest not to admit this: that heroin, at least to begin with, is very enjoyable. One of the first ex-addicts I talked to about heroin asked me to write the truth about this. Because young people won't trust you if you don't tell the truth, she said. Indeed, I became so accustomed to addicts and former addicts explaining to me that it was an experience of intense pleasure that I felt drawn to trying it out for myself.

There must be a "contagion effect" too, because the more I talked to heroin users about the drug, the more I felt this temptation to try it. The more I identified with the user, the more I felt drawn into a possible circle of complicity with them. The more I looked at the awful effects, and constant stories of early death, the more I understood the reasoning that something for which people risk life itself must be extraordinary. It was the good sense of my own sons, in their twenties, which pulled me back. They told me I would be mad and irresponsible even to think about it. After all the family had been through, after seeing their beloved cousins go to their graves, after all the suffering inflicted by heroin, how could I think of entertaining it? And with my own history of alcoholism, sampling such a highly addictive drug would be perilous. The director of a London recovery clinic, Michael Audreson of Rivendell, also warned me that you may open up "opiate receptors" in the central nervous system — by taking heroin — which may never be reversed.

Yet I do understand, fully, the allure. And when I told a friend of my own age (a middle-aged mother with a highly responsible job) about the initial effects of heroin — the reassurance, the comfort — she cried: "Get some! Ring a dealer now!" If heroin were legal, an awful lot more people would reach for it, since we live in an era where we expect to be comforted, we expect never to suffer, we expect a pill for every ill.

Most people who try heroin do so for the Mount Everest reason: because it is there. ("Why climb Mount Everest?" "Because it is there.") Many people start a habit just because it's around, and they like it. And some can indeed dabble in the drug for a short time, and then walk away from it. Vanessa, a cheerful and bubbly girl from an African diplomatic background, used heroin for about eighteen months in early adulthood (and, she added, when "her parents were too busy getting a divorce to notice" what she was doing). Like many others, she started on hash, and for her, from hash to heroin was a natural progression. As with many others, too, it was all just part of youthful experimentation. "You do everything when you're young, don't you? I was disillusioned with life in my twenties. I was very against the Establishment. They say you have to have thirty-two hits before you're an addict, and I was counting on having less than that."

It is my impression that women are better survivors in this, as in other matters. That they will not go in as deep, not abandon themselves quite as absolutely to the self-destructiveness of total heroin addiction. A few will, of course, especially if they start the habit very young, or if they are in a relationship which is heroin-based. The majority of young prostitutes are now said to be heroin users. But nothing like as many women die from heroin abuse as men, and the addiction rate itself never exceeds the ratio of one female for every three males.

There seems to be more resilience, and more powers of recovery in the female. "There's one girl I went out with who ended up as a cordon bleu chef," a Dublin guy recalls. "And she was just as bad a smack monster, if not worse, as the rest of us. But she just kind of shook it off. She was a heroin user without actually being an addict. She used for about two or three years. I run into her every now and again shopping in the supermarket and she is an impeccable surburban housewife. You would never know."

I believe that the maternal instinct in women, whether it is put to the use of maternity or not, acts as an inhibitor of the self-destructive urge: this, rather than social conditions alone, is the influential factor in the imbalance between male and female opiate use, as well as in suicides, where the imbalance is even more dramatic, disfavouring men. In all societies, men are more inclined to self-destruct than women.

There are recognised clinical factors now in identifying who is likely to become a heroin addict. There are, now, established danger signals. One is undoubtedly the loss of a parent, through death or divorce, at a crucial point of adolescence. It is "better", so to speak, to lose a parent, through divorce or death, as a young child, than at that intensely sensitive adolescent phase of thirteen, fourteen, fifteen, the vulnerable years.

If parents must get a divorce, it is preferable to do so either earlier, when the children are very young, or later, when they are adults, rather than at the cusp of their children's adolescence. The same, of course, goes for death, although in this we generally have less choice.

Many studies have also indicated that it is less of a disadvantage to be brought up by a single parent, from the start, than to lose a parent half-way into adulthood.

Dr John O'Connor, probably Ireland's most experienced expert in drug abuse, adds to the loss of a parent, "the absence of proper parenting". Parents who are too often absent; parents who have no "parenting skills"; parents who are too absorbed in their own lives; parents who drink and smoke excessively; and parents who are themselves subject to depression. In a study undertaken at the National Drugs Centre in Dublin, it was found that a quarter of girls with serious heroin problems had mothers who were themselves clinically depressed.

Blame the mothers! A good old Freudian tradition! These theories can be over-stated. Social history and biography show a much more nuanced and diverse view of child development. Most of us are not perfect parents, and most people, throughout history, have been imperfect parents. Individuals have grown up in appalling circumstances and have made good. Others have been brought up by model parents, and yet turned out helplessly neurotic. The human individual is made up of so many different parts, nurture, nature, heredity, chance, circumstances, environment, individuality, and peer group conformity.

Yet you do come across the pattern of parental loss in the life stories of heroin addicts, and sometimes of parental heedlessness.

One of the first recovering addicts I spoke to was Lucy, a young woman I knew very slightly: a mutual friend had told me of her former heroin habit. Like myself, Lucy had moved a lot between Dublin and London. Her family was Irish, and in financially comfortable circumstances. I had thought of her as a young woman with everything — looks, intelligence, money. I caught a glimpse of her once in a picture of a society wedding and thought, perhaps ungenerously, "How easy life is for these privileged young folk."

But Lucy was a typical vulnerable heroin type. She had adored her father, who died when she was twelve, and not untypical of teenage girls, was on a collision course with her mother by the time she was fourteen. From the age of fifteen, she was "always getting drunk". This was apparently tolerated in the circles in which she moved. "Nobody ever said to me, you drink too much." At the age of sixteen or seventeen, she was drinking whiskey regularly.

This is not unusual today. Before the cultural revolution of 1968, "nice" young people did not generally begin drinking until their late teens or early twenties. Girls at convent schools routinely "took the pledge" at their Confirmation, which formerly took place around the age of ten: this was expected to last until the age of twenty-one, and "breaking the pledge" before twenty-one was done guiltily, in defiance, or in the deliberate act of breaking a taboo. "Teenage hops" were run on lemonade: successful careers have been built on the proceeds of the "temperance ballrooms", which indicates that they were popular. But as counterculture values set in, youth drinking grew normalised. Young people seem so clever and sophisticated that, like sexual experience at an early age, it is usual to start drinking, and getting drunk, in adolescence.

It wasn't a big step, for Lucy, to move from whiskey to a variety of drugs. It started with cannabis; and the relative benevolence of cannabis makes teenagers distrust everything that the established order tells them about the drug culture. "Teenagers very quickly learn that what adults say isn't true." It isn't true that if you smoke cigarettes your health will immediately suffer: it takes thirty or forty years. It isn't true that if you smoke a joint, you'll develop throat cancer or terminal paranoia. And it isn't even true that if you try heroin you will immediately become addicted. Therefore, because teenagers distrust what adults tell them (and also see adults behave in a less than exemplary way) they brush aside health or drug education warnings.

And then, what gave Lucy a particular thrill about the experience of heroin (and cocaine, speed, and LSD, all of which she used in turn) was that it had the glamour of danger. "It's big, bad and dangerous. It's as bad as you can be. That's a great appeal." And then it was so much more satisfying than cannabis. "Everyone knows that smoking dope makes you boring. And silly. Heroin, on the other hand, makes you feel so confident — so at ease that you'll never feel right again without it."

For Lucy, it was the combination of being rather wild and wanting to test the boundaries. "Also, being very unhappy as a teenager. I very quickly learned how to use drink and drugs as a way to oblivion. I know I also used drink as a way of flirtatious behaviour with men. It gives you permission to behave badly.

"And like every other addict, I didn't think the rules applied to me. So I thought that I was the one who could take speed, take coke, never work, and pass all exams, never obey the rules of the road and never have car crashes; take heroin and not become an addict. I was shocked to realise that I had a physical habit."

In Alexander's case, the parental loss he endured really was terrible. A young man with soulful eyes and a faint, nervous stammer, he had some painful childhood experience of loss and discontinuity. "I was adopted by my grandparents and raised by them. They divorced when I was ten or eleven, but I stayed living with my adopted mother, that is, my grandmother.

"My natural mother was still around. Somewhere. My father actually died when I was very young. My natural mother had stayed with her parents, and then she remarried. This was something that I had a problem with — that my natural mother remarried, but left me with her parents.

"My grandparents were nice, yeah — particularly my grandmother. I wasn't particularly close to my grandfather, but I had no problem with him. Then they divorced and I continued to live with my grandmother."

So, by the age of ten, Alexander had undergone two traumas: a feeling of rejection by his biological mother, and the divorce of his adopted parents. A third and a fourth were then to strike. His grandmother developed breast cancer: she died when Alexander was fourteen. He looked after her for the last two years of her life. Within eighteen months his grandfather died of stomach cancer. Alexander went to live with some family friends, but really, from the age of fifteen, he was alone in the world. His mother did offer to take him, at this point, but he couldn't make the rapprochement. "I felt so hostile. I just felt that before she wanted me back, she had to wait for my grandmother to die."

Fifteen, as we know, is a very vulnerable age. It is the point of highest adolescent confusion, rebellion, and difficulty. At this age, Alexander was living in a bedsit in Canterbury, with some (very superficial) supervision from the local authority. Unsurprisingly, the experimentation with drugs began then. He quite quickly began dealing as well as using, since dealing is a way to support a drug habit. He feels "very, very bad" about this aspect of his drug career. He moved to Oxford and became heavily involved in supplying. "I now have a very big problem with this. It does actually bring me to tears, sometimes."

It was Alexander who helped me to understand that there aren't two separate compartments called "heroin users — victims of pushers" and "heroin dealers — evil pushers". Nearly all habitual heroin users are themselves dealers. And there is virtually no such thing as a heroin "pusher". You don't have to "push" heroin, alas. The market is ready and waiting. William Burroughs remarks in one of his books that far from the pusher trying to flog it, the user is anxiously "waiting for the man". Burroughs likens the approach of the dealer to the anticipation by the lover of the loved one. "You wait for his special step in the hall, his special knock, you scan the approaching faces on a city street. You can hallucinate every detail of his appearance as though he were standing there in the doorway." Being a dealer in heroin is empowering: it makes the user love you. Burroughs recalls the experience of "watching the play of hope and anxiety on the other's face, savouring the feeling of benevolent power, the power to give or withhold".

I have been sent many newspaper articles about "evil drug pushers" who "lure young people into drugs". Most of this is, frankly, drivel. Most young people try drugs eagerly, and when dependent, search desperately for their dealer. Lucy remembers the worst aspect of heroin use as waiting, waiting, waiting for the dealer to show. "I never met a so-called pusher. You have to try quite hard to get the drugs. They keep you waiting, they won't let you come when you want to. They're always paranoid. They change venues." (There is a book written about the drug culture actually called "Waiting for The Man" by Harold Shapiro.)

Alexander, as a former user and dealer — he has been clean for four years — doesn't "blame" his background, but he sees heroin as bridging an emotional gap, responding to an emotional need in his life. It comforted him. He still speaks of the habit as "comforting myself" or "indulging myself", as though it were a blanket he held onto.

But it wasn't only the loss that he had suffered before he was fifteen that made him vulnerable: it was also the lack of structures, the lack of authority. Other kids experimented with drugs at the same time as he did. He carried out all the early drug experiments — inevitably, again, beginning with cannabis — with his schoolfriends and peers. But they had a home to go back to. He remembers the others saying they had to clean themselves up, straighten themselves out, somehow, to appear at family supper. Xander had no boundaries either to test himself against, or even to defy. At the age of fifteen, he really could do as he pleased, and his school seemed as *laisser-faire* as everything else around him. Nobody even noticed, at school, that he was using, and dealing, in drugs.

"Too much authoritarianism" is sometimes given as a textbook reason for youthful addiction. "Over-authoritarian parents" are singled out as culprits. I do not dismiss the theory that reacting against authority is a powerful urge in the years of youthful energy and self-will. One of the reasons why I started drinking wildly in my twenties was that the habit helped me to maintain an attitude of rebellion against "the Establishment" (whatever that was). Getting drunk was thumbing your nose against all those bossy, respectable, law-and-order folk who made the rules. It was a way of cheeking back against all forms of authority — familial, the law, the moral order, and (as I saw it) male chauvinism. All those damn men who were always making rules about how we should live! Get outrageously drunk and shock the whole *galere*!

The great bourgeois virtue is "control". The sociological definition of middle-class values is the capacity for "deferred gratification". If you can defer a pleasure for a longer-term benefit (saving up for the future, investing in education), you are bourgeois. So let's do the opposite! Let's have some instant gratification! I want it now! Drunkenness meant being out of control and I liked that. I can perfectly identify with those for whom drugs performed a similar role.

And yet, I have not yet encountered a heroin addict who complained of over-strict parents (I have met some who complained of over-strict schools). My experience is that it is far more usual for a heroin user to be the child of liberal parents whose values were formed by the 1960s and who deplores "authoritarianism". Ben is like this. A bright, sparky art teacher in his twenties — a brilliant academic who got a first and then a masters — he is open and warm.

We found it easy to be friendly, because he seems an easy person. Yet there was a lot of pain in his early life. He is the only child of his parents' union (he does have older half-siblings).

He loves his parents. He sees them regularly. But they were "let-it-all-hang-out" *soixante-huitards* (the French slang for those who came of age in 1968). They were not strong on "authoritarian" moral frameworks. They were also inconsistent. Ben saw more violence than he cares to dwell on. There'd be violent arguments, and then there'd be hugs all round.

Whether by nature or by formation, Ben describes himself as "totally insecure and self-destructive. I latch on to hero types, people who are larger than life. Mythical kinds of figures. Burroughs, for example." The writer William Burroughs, who died at the age of eighty-three after a lifelong heroin habit, is an iconic figure in heroin culture. Yet this need for the heroic is also highlighted in an unusual Jungian study of heroin addicts, which sees opiates as a replacement for the ritualised and heroic element of culture we have lost in a more banalised, utilitarian and de-sacrilised society. There are no epic heroes any more: except, perhaps, significantly in *Star Wars* and its equally successful prequel *The Phantom Menace*.

The true hero must struggle with life-and-death forces, writes this Jungian, Dr Luigi Zoja. (This theme has been taken up more recently by the mythologist Joseph Campbell, who affirms man's need for fable, myth and heroism.) "The main characteristic of the hero's battle in its purest and most archetypal form is the fact that he puts his very existence at stake, that he fights wholeheartedly to either win or die. But in our modern world, where every acrobat is assured of a safety net beneath him, such an experience has been relegated to the unconscious." Dr Zoja even suggests that the practice of duelling, regarded by the enlightened (and by Christians) as a terrible nineteenth century scourge which needlessly took the life of young men, might have psychically satisfied the need for heroism, and thus prevented worse scourges — like heroin addiction. I scarcely think that we are likely to have a return to duelling, but it might be worth studying the initiation rites of passage which have marked adolescent transitional experience in many, many societies, yet which we have lost.

Ben admits that he "loved heroin". He loved the feeling of warmth, a point often made by users. Before using heroin, he'd been "shooting up speed and coke, taking loads of pills before that, so heroin didn't worry me — at first". Heroin has the heroic element of bringing you to the edge, to the total extreme. That exhilarated Ben at the beginning. (With heroin — everything is "at the beginning".) "Once you've done heroin, yeah, once you've been there and done it and got really high, you look back on the other drugs, and you think, 'recreational drugs' with a kind of contempt. Heroin — it's a different league. Long-term, it's the worst thing in the world. You've got to be a moron to do it. There's parts of us that are morons."

There are heroin addicts with ghastly backgrounds: no question about it. Rosina, a North Dubliner, lost both a sister and a brother to heroin — both died, one of AIDS. A second sister is now HIV (from a very brief affair with an addict who had AIDS, and has since died), and a younger brother, now abroad, is also using heroin. Her mother was a Traveller (that is, from the nomadic Irish people once called Tinkers, as distinguished from hippies who take to the road) who married into settled life. But the home was riddled with conflict, and, according to Rosina, her mother was neglectful. Rosina's sister, now dead, was also given Valium "to keep her quiet" as a child, rather as heedless mothers fed laudanum — a tranquillising concoction of opium and alcohol — to their babies in the nineteenth century, from which many infants died.

With women addicts, sexual abuse has been identified as a likely factor in childhood, by expert studies (although women addicts will not always choose heroin: various cocktails of pills can be the female "drug of choice".) John, a successful Dublin businessman had a much-loved sister, Sandra. She was "the life and soul of the party" type, he recalls. She developed a drug habit, and in the course of counselling, it emerged that another brother had violated her from the age of eleven to her mid-teens: penetration and oral sex were both involved. John wanted Sandra to press charges against their brother, and the matter hung in the balance for some time. Then Sandra took her own life, using barbiturates. Sandra's mother died soon after that, as a consequence of self-neglect. After these deaths, it further emerged that there had also been sexual abuse from her father. Strangely, prior to these revelations, John had always perceived his family to be decent, happy, and respectable.

Some nuns and priests involved in pastoral care see the heroin epidemic as inextricably linked with the fragmentation of home life which has taken place in recent years, a contributing factor also underlined by the American social analyst, Fukuyama. "Sure, there's no home life!" says Brother Alfonso, a friar at St Mary of the Angels Church in central Dublin. He points to the nearby municipal flats in the vicinity of the church. "The fathers aren't there! The mothers aren't there! There are no regular meals! There's no home life. Why wouldn't the youngsters be on drugs?" This was a theme much emphasised by Victorian temperance campaigners: that drunkenness was linked with the absence of domestic order, and also caused such family deterioration. A quirky, and beneficial, outcome of the temperance movement's interest in a good home life was their promotion of early twentieth-century do-it-yourself home improvements.

Yet, you meet all kinds of people who develop an addiction to heroin. I spent a lovely summer evening having dinner with a colleague, a writer, in Notting Hill Gate: his home life had been fine – his father is a distinguished medical specialist, his mother educated and conscientious. Jamie was one of two, well-planned children and he could not identify any major unhappiness in his childhood. He thought his father a little remote, perhaps. He thought his mother probably preferred his sister, as a child, because she was quiet and diligent, whereas Jamie was lively and playful. His prep school was strict – too strict – and expected high results, which were generally forthcoming. But there were no real problems, no significant childhood trauma.

Jamie got to Oxford, and there started experimenting with drugs. He just liked the feeling. He had always felt "different" as a child — something that is very often expressed by people at Alcoholic Anonymous meetings — and drugs helped him to "fit in". Heroin helped him cope, essentially, with boredom. He has used a cocktail of drugs throughout his twenties, including Prozac — the popular "happiness drug", launched in 1987 — and Seroxat, an anti-depressant. Both had been prescribed for him when he felt blue. He has also used alcohol extensively. Jamie, in his thirties, struggles with his drug use: he is on and off, on and off. He cannot rid himself of a feeling of "low self-esteem" — first identified by Alfred Adler as "the inferiority complex" — and yet his mother says that his real problem is that he was just too clever. "Jamie, you think too much."

I have met long-term heroin users who cannot speak highly enough of their background and upbringing: who had no trauma at all in their childhood that they can recall. Tom, now in his fifties, says he had a lovely childhood. His parents were working-class, and unusually liberal for their time. "They were very nice people. I couldn't have had nicer parents," he says. "They were free-thinkers. No prejudice towards anyone, whether coloured people, any nationality, drug addicts or prostitutes. There's good in everyone as far as they are concerned. They tried to make sure we did our homework and that, but they never beat us or anything."

His parents were married in 1947, and again, unusually for the time and their milieu, they lived together before getting married — a custom only practiced at that time by arty Bohemians or the politically conscious, "making a statement" against bourgeois standards. Tom still visits his father every week, and cares for him if the old man is unwell — his mother is now dead.

Yet Tom, a session musician, started experimenting with drugs at the age of twelve — he took Mandrax (the methaqualone drug, now unavailable) which made him "pharmaceutically aware". Heroin made him feel heroic, and comfortable. In the end, it gave him up: all his veins are retracted and he cannot use heroin any more. He needs methadone to maintain stability. Most heroin addicts, it is said, either die, or stop, but some continue using and survive to live a normal life-span. Tom has survived, but still there is a price. There is a dreary round of methadone collection, and dosage; plus the anxiety about travel, lest one should be separated from the methadone supply.

Lucy knows a couple of very rich heroin users who have never had problems with procurement, and have been able to survive over thirty or forty years without detriment to their health. "But it does narrow your life down, and your emotions freeze. You become very very narrow. I have a cousin by marriage who is extremely rich, and he has been addicted for twenty years. He remains like a teenager. It closes down your ability to develop as a character, or to develop other interests."

It has to be accepted that some individuals try heroin simply because it is available." Availability is the major determinant," writes John Boothe Davis, who is head of a Scottish addiction institution. "Most people who use drugs do so for their own reasons, on purpose, because they like it, because they find no adequate reasons for not doing so ..." "At first, at least, we do it because we like it, and we like it because it is nice," writes Tam Stewart in a much-praised autobiographical account of heroin use.

Undoubtedly, the peer group is a major influence. The "peer group" has now become as crucial a factor, arguably, in psychological formation as parental power.

A recent study of child development, *The Nurture Assumption*, by Judith Rich Harris, claims that in Western society now, the peer group, rather than the parents, are the "primary agents of socialisation".

Paul, a working-class Yorkshireman who used heroin solidly for fifteen years, had a very typical "peer group" start. "Everyone" was beginning to experiment around 1981 or 1982, among his friends. Another friend gave Paul some heroin for his eighteenth birthday. "It seemed perfectly normal. I was getting used to this kind of drug culture then. And it was giving people new experiences." He was proud to be among the second or third in the circle of friends to try it. Paul, incidentally, also had an extremely supportive father who never reproached him once, even when he served a prison sentence for possession, but visited him regularly and tried only to give him kindly guidance. Paul married in his twenties, and he and his young wife were regulars at rock festivals, where drugs were easily available.

"Most young users," writes Charles Faulpel in an American academic study of heroin, "were turned on by close friends who were themselves experimenting." The use of heroin in the group "was seen as an expression of trust, friendship and acceptance. Most lower-strata youth were introduced to drugs by a close friend or relative. After they learned to use drugs for pleasure, being turned on and turning others on became an established social practice, similar to the convention of buying a friend a drink or offering a drink to a guest when he comes to your house."

Experimentation with drugs is now part of youth culture, especially since experimentation with sex is no longer seen as outrageous or daring. Sexual activity has become so accepted, even so regulated and commercialised, that it holds little echo of rebellion. "Sex is neither shocking nor illegal but drugs are both," observed Vicki Woods writing in the Sunday Telegraph. But the question of whose personality will draw them further into a destructive downward spiral of drug addiction is more complex, I believe. Sometimes an over-logical or an over-rational analysis does not perceive the mystical and even cabalistic aspect of heroin lives. I spent an evening with an Anglo-Polish heroin user, Marek, in which the conversation ranged from astrology to the works of Carlos Castenada. Marek told me I should "see with my ears and hear with my eyes", for the ears are feminine and the eyes masculine and the masculine-feminine interchange must take place for insightful symmetry.

He said that I should familiarise myself with "Chyron, the Wounded Healer" and that I would never penetrate the enigma of heroin until I had understood that the mystery of the universe was contained in the letter Seven. I would need to be part of a secret cabalistic world to comprehend this. I do not disparage the strange and the mystical: it is also part of human experience which reason alone cannot appreciate. I came away with a certain sense of the occult, but no wiser.

Some artistic people also seek in heroin a source of creative inspiration. The writers Coleridge, De Quincey, Francis Thompson, Wilkie Collins and Keats took opium (as did, surprisingly, the great slave liberator, William Wilberforce, though he had the unusual strength of character never to increase the small, regular dose), and some writers and artists think that heroin, today's equivalent, will also open the doors of poetry and perception. But in a celebrated study of nineteenth century literary addicts, "Opium and the Romantic

Imagination," Alethea Hayter concluded that opiates are more likely, in the end, to stultify creative achievement than to inspire it. "The intention, but failure, to write a great philosophical work is a regular feature in the biography of addict writers." De Quincey's compelling autobiography is marked by the fragmented thinking which typifies drug use.

Miss Hayter identifies three characteristics which predisposed individuals towards opiate addiction. (She excludes the question of family predilection, which was not considered important in the early nineteenth century, before Darwin and Freud.) One was a restless curiosity about strange and novel mental experiences, a fascination with "altered states".

The second was a longing for peace, for freedom from anxiety and pain, and certain inadequacies in the personality in facing "real life". And the third was an attraction for secret societies of any kind, for rite and rituals and for hidden fellowships. Opium is not heroin: it was taken in droplets, not syringes, and many aspects of the drug culture have changed. But those three individual characteristics still hold true, it seems to me.

Mary Kenny

Letter from Keith

I'd be more than willing to help you to understand the terrible destruction heroin brings, not just only to yourself, but your family and everybody who lives around you.

Heroin is after making me jump over shop counters and robbing nearly every single thing in sight of it. It has me in prison, also methadone is no solution either. For me there is only one solution and that's the power of my brain. In the last three weeks, and this is no exaggeration, three friends have died by overdose from heroin. At the moment I'm doing fifteen months, but I've a lot of more serious charges to face in the courts. I've been coming to prison since I've been seventeen. I'm twenty-six now, and I'd say I've spent two years altogether outside "free".

My parents got me a doctor to help us get off the heroine (sic), by giving us — me and my girlfriend — a methadone course. Started that and stayed off the heroine (sic) for about three to four months. Missed it, abused my methadone by starting to take heroine on top of my methadone. Sharon did, got a job with a top hairdressers. Start to doing good in work while my day would be going to get money for heroine. Until I got this sentence in prison, at the moment am still off drugs and I'm doing my very best to stay off them as I know if I don't, I'll be in prison till I die. I've also seen a lot of Deaths in the community caused by heroine. It's a real nightmare. I hope you'll get a better understanding of it by this letter. So, be good, and bye bye,

Keith. Mountjoy Prison.

Chapter Five

Lauren, Aged Sixteen:
An Experiment with Death

It was once considered "deviant" for a young person to experiment with drugs. It is now, statistically, considered to be normal. Young people will probably do so, around the age of sixteen — many earlier. But it is still a shock for parents to discover that the drug their child has experimented with is heroin.

When Annette Rodgers found that her daughter Lauren had tried heroin at the age of fifteen, she did what she could to try and save Lauren from dependence on the drug, including, at one point, buying street heroin to keep her daughter safely at home. It still ended in tragedy.

Annette is forty-three, with a young and wholesome face. She lives in Derby, where she works with a charity. Lauren was her eldest child: she also has two sons. Annette is divorced, though her former husband lives nearby, and they had an amicable arrangement over the children. Annette has come to believe that a heroin addict is born with the addiction; but that young people are made more vulnerable by growing up too fast, getting too much too soon.

'People feel ashamed to talk about this problem. But for Lauren's sake, I feel I have to be open about it now.

I discovered Lauren's diary, in which she had written that she tried heroin, and that it was "wicked". Obviously I screamed and shouted, but that didn't do any good. She broke down crying. I confronted her about it. She said, will you help me to get off it, I can't get off it, it's controlling me. She did recognise that. She did ask for help. So I said I would help, but I needed to find out more about it.

I needed to know more about it. I wanted to know what it was, what does it look like. It cost £10 a time, and her boyfriend was doing it too. They bought it together, whoever they got the money off, they sold a couple of things — my engagement ring that I'd had from her father. And she said, I'm going to make an appointment to go to the GP, and I said, OK, you do that. She went to the GP and he said, all right, I'll refer you. A lot of GPs are very ignorant about it. A junkie — go away, get out of my surgery sort of thing ....

A drug-addict is a drug-addict. They're not the person that they used to be.

Yet she was sweet — when she'd just scored. She did everything for me, then. We were the best of friends. She'd clean the house, she'd have my tea ready when I came home. When she was withdrawing and she needed the money — she was a totally different person. She was going through adolescence as well. It was just such a struggle for her. To go through that and to go through drugs. Awful.

She started heroin on 18 December 1997. It was in her diary. Six months and she was dead.

Since she was thirteen, I'd had problems with her anyway. She was truanting from school. She wasn't interested. She knew everything. She was a rebellious teenager. The school wasn't interested. Here, a pupil disrupts the class too much and they're excluded. It's nothing new. It's been going on for years. But you weren't thrown out in the past. They used to stop my sport, stop me doing something I liked. Now they won't take the trouble. As soon as a child is in school, it's the responsibility of the school to get them disciplined, not throw them out.

We're very open in our house, and we used to sit and talk about drugs. I used to talk about heroin and I used to say, now you do realise that heroin is the end of the line, don't you? I'm young in my outlook. We talked about it. She was a very headstrong, powerful girl anyway.

She wasn't going to school, but I didn't think she was daft enough to take heroin. She had a welfare officer, but he was a waste of time. Wasn't interested. But in Derby, there's an alternative to school called Step Forward, where kids go where they have had problems at school. It's a relaxed atmosphere, they're talked to, instead of at. She did go every day. She had been a very, very clever girl at primary school. She'd been a model pupil, as a little girl. Something changed with Lauren when she was about eleven or twelve.

She knew a bad crowd, yes. Yes. Definitely. She used to seek these people out. Her father, he came up with this theory — we're on very good terms, generally — he came up with the theory, that she hated competition. When she was with somebody who wasn't in competition with her, she was in charge, she was the leader, and that was OK. But once she wasn't the leader, once she had competition, she felt that as a blow to her esteem. I could quite go with that theory. You do think you know everything at fifteen, sixteen.

This is awful to say about your own daughter, but we were also worried about Lauren being a bad influence on other people. Because she was so strong. The boyfriend was on it, too, of course. Wrong place, wrong time, with the wrong people. She was sixteen that November. Sixteen. He was twenty-one. He was a really, really nice boy. His mother threw them both out, because they were staying there, so they came to live with us. So there was Lauren and him. They were both heroin addicts. He hasn't stopped, I've heard.

In the end, I just fully understood what was happening to her, and just went along with it. Though I felt very angry at times.

I've got a best friend whose son is a heroin addict. He started at the same time as Lauren. I see her every week, she sobs in my arms, she doesn't know what to do. He runs off, you see. Once they get some money, they go off for days. Disappear. That's what Lauren used to do. But I never worried. I just used to think, well I know what she's doing. She'll be back. Sure enough, as soon as the money run out, she was back.

My eldest son knew about it. The younger didn't. I said to her if I find any trace in the house, that you are using in the house, you're out. You must not use in the house, while any of us are there. When I went to the GP, he referred us to a drugs clinic in Derby. She wanted to go. She wanted to come off it.

I found out in the January. And we went to the doctors in February. And we were seen straight away by this counsellor. She went along with all that, completely. We used to go to the counsellor, and I would go as well.

When she went, he said, how do you want to do this: cold turkey, which is where you come off completely. You go warm turkey, which is where you are given painkillers, then sleeping tablets ... or methadone? Then I said I didn't want her to have methadone, because you're replacing one drug with another. And then she said, I want to go into hospital. I want to go away. And he said, right, we'll get you into detox. We waited seven weeks. And he said to me, because she's chosen to go into hospital, there's no alternative. That's it. Until she goes into detox, she'll continue using heroin.

So: we got to the point where she'd be asking for money every day, and it was £10 a day, £15 a day or whatever. This particular day she said, she could get a good deal. She'd been ripped off by a dealer. If you give me £30 it could keep us going for six days. And I thought, that would be nice, not having any pressure over money for six whole days.

So I said, I'm doing the deal. I need the pressure off me for six days. She thought it was highly amusing that her mum wanted to do the deal. So I went to this estate in Derby. It's horrid. They all live round there. But he was a heroin addict himself, the dealer. Word soon got round that Lauren's mum had done a deal. He was a pathetic character, awful. I was sorry for him. I thought, at least she's got me. He's got nobody. Anyway I left her there. I said, this has got to last. I don't want you going on a binge ....

Afterwards I thought, what am I doing? I left her there in the estate to do what she had to do. I didn't want her doing it in the house. I said, I want you back home tonight, and I want to see how much you've used. I'm serious. She did. She kept her word.

Lauren was a junkie with standards. I know that's a contradiction. She used to go for HIV tests. Hepatitis tests at the local hospital. She used to go to the needle exchange — she always used to use clean needles. She was a very sensible junkie. She was just very sensible. When she died everything was in place. She even had a neat little drawer where she kept condoms. She was very fastidious.

The only indication was the spoons. They have to mix it with baking soda, something like that. Then they burn on a spoon so that it goes into a liquid, and draw it into the needle. All my spoons disappeared. And I said to her, I don't want the younger boy knowing what's going on. He's only eleven. She was very reasonable.

She had her moments. We'd sort of carry on as normal as you can be. One day, when I came home from work, I went into the house, her boyfriend had got all his stereo equipment out. There were people in the house — they were negotiating the price to buy this stereo. I told them to get out of the house, and there was an enormous row. I'm losing control of my own house, and this has got to stop. They got £150 for the hi-fi, they were ripped off over that too.

I used to hide money under the mattress. I had a bag for my valuables, she stole that. Scott's wallet. That's my partner. She stole Scott's credit card, tried to use it, and she couldn't. I said, do it to me, Laurie, but don't do it to Scott. He doesn't deserve it. He's not family. She cried and cried. And she wrote him a wonderful letter, saying how sorry she was. She never touched a penny of his after that. Her moral faculties were still working.

I never repeated that deal with the dealer. He owed too much money out to the big guys, and he stopped dealing, he was going out robbing to get heroin. It's Asians who usually deal in Derby. Blacks won't deal in heroin. It's not something that they get into, because they know that it kills.

We eventually got the letter to go into detox and she did. In the beginning of April — it had taken about nine weeks. She went in for two weeks. Near Nottingham. And after the two weeks, she said, I want to come home. She followed the programme — with a lot of heartache, but she did it. I couldn't visit for seven days. But when I went to visit she kept calling me Mummy. This being more babyish than Mum. Reverted to a more childlike state. Like to be a child now. Her letters are all "Mummy, Mummy."

She had a keyworker — somebody that looks after them. They thought there that she was too young for counselling. Yet she had seen far too much for a sixteen-year-old girl. Her keyworker said she had never had a patient who was so intelligent. "She's the most sensible junkie I've ever seen. We can't get over it, she's only sixteen. She'll be all right."

She was fine, when she came out. She cut her hair really short. She looked very nice. She looked alive. She got all the colour back in her cheeks. No spots. Her periods came back. And she was wonderful. That was May 1. We moved into our new house on May 2, and she came out of detox on May the first. This was 1998.

She'd got a flat. I wanted her to come home, but no, she wanted to go and live with her boyfriend; she wanted to have her flat. I said you must contact me every day. So she decorated the flat very nicely, lots of ornaments. Her boyfriend got it through the probation service. It was round the corner from her dad. He is on his own. They had a very, very fiery relationship. They're very much alike. And they were always falling out. And when we first found out she was a heroin addict, he wouldn't have anything to do with her at all.

He said, she's no daughter of mine. Until in the end, I couldn't cope any longer financially, and with the pressure, and so I rang him up and begged him to help us, and he said, yes, OK, I will. And he was totally different then, I made him understand what was happening with her. She then said, Oh Dad, please help, I need help. So that was it. So she was all right in May. Fine. She had her own flat. I used to visit regularly.

She was due to leave school. The day she died, some letters arrived at her father's house for some interviews, to go on a training course. She said, I want to be like you, Mum, I want to work in an office. She didn't have any specific ambitions, no. She just wanted a job. She felt she had wasted her life, and she wanted to do something.

Then about three weeks after she came out of detox, I took them shopping. I knew they'd scored. I could tell by the way John spoke. And I could just tell by her attitude. My heart sank, it was awful. And we went shopping and we got back to the car. And I said, "you've scored", and she said no, you think I'd waste all that money. And I said, look at me and tell me you haven't. We had a row. I said to John, you've scored today, haven't you? He'd cleaned himself up, done cold turkey. He had done really well. But I could tell more with him, because he used to fall asleep. He gave the game away. I just knew they had scored.

A few days after that, she came to meet me from work — we used to go for coffee. I said to her, you did score last week, didn't you? She sat and cried again, I said, just

106

be honest with me, please, I can cope with anything as long as you're honest. OK, she said. I'm sorry, I'm sorry. I said, why, after all you've been through, to hell and back. She said I just wanted to see if I could control it, instead of it controlling me.

I suppose, when you hit a low, you think, well, I know what will make me feel better.

Coming out of detox, though, she didn't have any group to go to. It was just like, off you go now. She was given some drugs, a blocker which blocks the receptors for craving, so she was to take one of those every two days. If she tried heroin, she wouldn't get a buzz out of it. She took them, then didn't take them. Then did take them. And I'd never been able to understand why, until recently, it came to me. It's the idea that you have one more fix, before you really stop. It's the idea that you can feel really good for just one day, before you quit.

Yes, I did give her money. She started borrowing from me. But I thought it was for the flat, which she really liked to decorate with little ornaments. Mostly they lived on his Giro. But she would never ask for exactly £10, because we both knew that was the price of a hit.

The week that she died, she met me on the Wednesday. She'd been to counselling, then, but I couldn't go with her. I had such a lot on at work, she was on her own, she'd had a big fallout with her boyfriend, who had nearly OD'd a couple of weeks before, while she wasn't there. She'd gone to stay with a friend. And she started looking poorly again, and I said to her, you're not eating, you look awful. She said, I've got my period.

We'd had by then got a counsellor, and we were both having counselling. So the counsellor said, so what would you do if Lauren went back to heroin. And I said,

I would have to cut her free, I would have to cut the ties because I cannot cope with Lauren and heroin again, I've got to think of myself and the rest of the family. This time, I said to Lauren, you choose heroin or you choose your family. You can't choose both.

She just said OK. And then on the Wednesday, she met me for lunch. In counselling, she was really, really upset, really, really low ... nothing was going right for her. She said, I've got to get out of the flat, 'cause John wasn't there. She said, I'm moving back into Dad's at the weekend. So I said, oh, things will be fine at your Dad's. Anyway, she didn't have lunch, she wouldn't eat anything. I said, you're looking awful, and then I thought, she's back into something. I left her at the chemist, to go and get Naltrexone (the opiate blockers).

I said to her, I love you Laurie, ... what's the matter? She said, nothing's going right. She said, if I had £100, I'd buy a load of gear and I'd die. But I'd die very happy. I said, please don't do that to me. I'd never give up on you. Please don't do that to me. Oh, she said, I'm just fed up, and that was it. I said, I'll see you later, give me a ring. When you've seen your Dad. She said, yes, OK. I said, am I seeing you tomorrow? She said, not tomorrow, John gets his Giro, we're going out for the day. I said, OK, that's something to do. I said, come and see me at work on Friday, and she said, OK, I will. With that, off she went.

On Thursday, her Dad rang me, and said Lauren's got some letters here at the house, will you see her later? No, I said, she's out with John for the day, he's got his Giro. I'll ring his mum's later. I got home from work, I rang, no answer, I thought she's out with John. I thought nothing of it. Friday came, and I was just so busy at work, and I usually finish at three on a Friday and I was there till six.

I said to my colleague, that's unusual, Lauren usually comes here on a Friday. So I rang her Dad's and there was no answer. Her Dad used to take her sometimes out to tea. He wasn't in. Rang John's house, nobody in.

Saturday morning I got up, and I just had this really, really bad feeling, and I thought, got to see Lauren today, got to see her. Had this really sick feeling. I was going up to see my Mum, I took the older boy. She said, are you all right, where's Madam, what's Madam doing? I don't know, haven't seen her since Wednesday, bit worried because she's not been in touch.

Left my mother's, went back to the flat, still no answer, got Steve, her dad, and I said, I don't suppose you've heard from Lauren and he said, I've not spoken to her since Wednesday. And God, I said, I've not heard from her. I rang John, and he said, I've not seen her since Wednesday. I said, she was supposed to go out with you for the day. I know, he said. We called round but there was no answer. Maybe she's gone off with her mate, to get her own back on me, to make me jealous.

This friend had not seen her for two weeks. I said, something's going on. This was now two o'clock in the afternoon. I went to the flat again, it was a big house. The lad upstairs hadn't seen her since Wednesday. There was no other key. You had to go to an office outside of Derby to get an extra key.

All this time, I knew. As soon as I got back home from my Mum's, I knew. I got back in the car, and I sobbed, and Steve said: what're you crying for? And I said, she's dead. I knew it. He said, don't be stupid. I said, I just know it. She's in there, she's dead. They wouldn't believe me.

Just opposite where they live, there's a carnival ...
Seven o'clock at night, still nobody could get it. Finally,
the manageress was coming over with a key, at eight-
thirty.

I said, there's no way I'm going in that flat, because
you'll find my daughter dead. I said, you're going to find
a dead girl. My friend and her husband went in, and I
stayed outside with Scott. Then he went in, and I just
stood outside. The next thing he just opened the door and
he looked at me. I said, she is dead, isn't she? He didn't
say anything, he just looked at me. He said, the
ambulance is coming ... they told him not to say anything
to me. Then my friend Bernie came out, and she said, Oh
Annette ... I went hysterical then.

They pronounced her dead that day, 6th June. But
really, she died a couple of days beforehand. I didn't go
into the flat. They wouldn't let me. That night, we had to
go to the mortuary. It was horrible. Her eyes were open.
I suppose they'd have had to break everything. She was
curled on up the settee. The needle was still in her arm.
She must have just gone to sleep. She took a fatal
overdose.

I honestly believe she wanted out. And that was her
way of getting out. Because it had started to take over her
life again. And she thought, well, I've lost my boyfriend...
I have no prospects. Out on the bed was her CV, all typed
out. All laid out on the bed. So that people knew who she
was. And she kept a diary, herself. On the Monday it said,
please let me die, I want to die. On the Wednesday, she'd
only written half of it. Teenagers, they get very depressed
anyway.

With her, everything had to be instant. Otherwise, she
had no life. If it wasn't instant, then she couldn't see.

The funeral service was beautiful. So many young people.

Had to clear the flat out. I took back her little jewellery box. The younger boy talks to this little jewellery box with her ashes in it. That's her shrine.

There is no fighting it. There is really no fighting heroin at all. It is so powerful.

The reason why? Curiosity. Boredom. Bravado. Peer pressure. And it's too readily available. Far too readily available.

I had to ring Colin, at the clinic. He couldn't believe it. He said, she was my star pupil. He had said, I'd have put money on Lauren making it. He couldn't believe it.

She was thirteen when her dad and I broke up. I asked her did she blame me, and she said, no, I don't blame you at all. She actually told me I'd got to leave. Mum, she said, you'll have to leave. But we did it quite amicably. I gave her the choice as to who she'd live with. But he has so much guilt now.

There was no drinking in the family. His parents were the nicest people. They didn't know, until she died, about the heroin. They knew she was a problem. She used to adore them as a small child.

Lauren had a ring in her nose. She had shaved her hair off. No, I didn't mind that. You have to go along with fashions. I was a very liberal parent. What's the point of trying to fight it?

Yet she grew up too fast. Everything was too fast. She was on the Pill. She had condoms and clean needles neatly ranged in her flat. She didn't want to smoke. "I don't want to ruin my lungs." As I say, she was a junkie with standards. Yet she felt "warm and safe" with heroin.

She used to speak about God in her letters. She wrote loads of poems. She was so deep. She left a lot of writing. She left a letter, to a friend of mine, who had a lot of bad fortune, and she said, you have such a crap life, what you need is an angel to guide you, and very soon you will have that angel to guide you through your life. Lauren became the angel.

She used to say: "I'm so sorry I've let you down." But in some cases, there is just nothing you can do. You've got to be able to understand. You've got to be non-judgemental. Yet I was relieved when Lauren died. She was never going to come out of it. Heroin addicts — Mary, they're born.'

Part II

Chapter Six

The Decision to Recover

The addict has to want to help themselves. That is the key factor in the decision to recover.
— Diana Wells, clinic director.

When you give up junk, you give up a way of life. Why does a junky quit junk of his own will? You never know the answer to that question...The decision to quit junk is a cellular decision, and once you have decided to quit you cannot go back to junk permanently any more than you could stay away from it before.
— William Burroughs, *Junky*.

It has to be the addict's decision to quit. That was emphasised to me again, and again. No one else can do it for him. Forcing someone into treatment is unlikely to work. Until the addict is genuinely ready to make the commitment, he is likely to emerge from the most comprehensive and expensive treatment, and go straight back to addiction. Even when he has made the commitment, genuinely, he may relapse several times. Addiction is sometimes defined as a relapsing disorder.

But there are moments, epiphanies, opportunities, lucky breaks and good timing when some kind of intervention helps. I consider my own experience with alcohol, which is not the same as heroin (it takes longer to kill you, it is legal, and we are acculturated to it), but the inability to control drink nonetheless has something in common with a compulsive heroin habit. Somebody was kind enough to say to me, "Mary — have you ever considered that you might have a drink problem?" Did I listen? No, not at all, at the time. I was enraged, outraged, insulted, indignant. I called the man — a mere acquaintance — every kind of a busybody and male chauvinist pig ("you're only saying that because I'm a woman"). He smiled wryly and no more was said. But something must have drip-dripped into my consciousness, and some years later I was grateful to that man. It was a kind thing to do. It was a responsible thing to do. It was the opposite of the shoulder-shrugging existentialist "it's-her-choice" indifference. I rebuffed it at first, but it made a difference.

So while it must be the individual's decision to quit, people have been helped, nudged, encouraged, put on the right road by the right intervention at the right time. At the Merchant's Quay project in Dublin, probably the best-known drop-in centre for addicts and their families in Ireland, it has been known for an addict to be brought along by their employer: and the intervention has helped. But then an addict who is in employment is already at an advantage: over 85 per cent of addicts are unemployed. An addict whose employer has taken the trouble to help him must feel he is valued by the employer.

With a young addict, the pro-active intervention of a parent or family member can be very successful, if the timing is right. For Lucy, a young woman who used heroin — "fiercely" — in both Dublin and London, as I described in Chapter Four — the pressure from a strong-minded mother, coinciding with a sense in herself, that she was spiralling downwards into more and more unhappiness, clinched the decision. "I always thought that I took drugs because I was unhappy. I hadn't realised that I was unhappy because I was taking drugs." Lucy was doing drugs with her boyfriend, a not unusual pattern with women, but her life was coming apart, in her twenties. "I had no money. I had no job. I was desperate. I was feeling ill a lot of the time."

At this crucial point her mother found out about her habit, though Lucy thinks now that, sub-consciously, she wanted her mother to know. "My behaviour was pretty odd. I was unreliable. I'd disappear ... I wasn't where I was supposed to be a lot of the time."

Her mother came on with a strong dose of "tough love". She cut off all financial help to her daughter, and started suggesting a range of rehabilitation clinics. Lucy tried several, which were no help to her. There are some bad rehab clinics, Lucy says. Or there are some which help some people but are useless for others. Finally, she was booked into a rehab in the West of England which turned out to be right for her.

Rehab clinics de-toxify the addict — that is, remove the opiates and drugs from their system — and then seek to help them get off addiction to the drug on a more permanent basis, using a variety of therapies. It is socially unfair, and unjust, that people with the means to book into a clinic can do so, whereas poorer addicts do not have that choice — though there is a trend to open up more public beds, funded by local authorities or the health authority, and this ought to be a feature of political policy. Health authority hospitals, in Ireland and the UK, may also do detoxifications.

But detoxification alone will hardly ever cure a heroin addict. Something else has to be added.

The rehab clinic's approach suited Lucy because other therapies, including psychotherapy, had simply not worked for her. "The trouble with any kind of analysis is that I started feeling more justified in taking drugs. I felt even more sorry for myself. But here they just said, 'Look, we don't really want to know about the fact that your father died, and your mother wasn't around and that you were desperately unhappy as a teenager. But what we can tell you is that you've been taking far too many drugs for a number of years. And we're going to tell you how to stop. That's your problem. We're not really concentrating on your other problems.' That was right for me. It was very tough. It made me take responsibility for myself."

Lucy now thinks that "the way to help an addict, I'm afraid, is to make their lives very unpleasant. You allow them to suffer the consequences of their actions. You even allow them to get arrested by the police. The pain has got to be greater than the pleasure. The downside of taking drugs has got to be worse than the upside.

"When you're a heroin user," she reflects, "you get away with it for so long. People tolerate bad behaviour. Your unreliability is tolerated. Your morality goes, as one taboo after another gets broken." The rehab worked, and she got clean. That was now a decade ago: she split up from the heroin boyfriend, got married to a nice man, and is the mother of several young children.

An event which has jolted some addicts into recovery is — getting arrested by the police. It comes as a horrible shock to a young person who is not familiar with the criminal justice system: it will have little, or less, impact on an individual who has been previously in trouble with the law, or who mixes in circles where the police, and the law, are regarded in a hostile or critical manner anyway.

But police intervention is frightening to two groups of heroin users: those who have a definite cultural background of respecting law and order, who fear the loss of respectability, and detest the "hassle" involved in court appearance. And those people who want to do well in their jobs and do not want to "screw up" a promising career with a drug conviction. My nephew Conor, who people I've encountered in the film business believed had a brilliant future as a film-maker, would probably have benefited from a stern caution by a garda officer. Respectability wouldn't have worried his artistic soul, but the thought of harming his film prospects might well have pulled him up from such risky recreations.

It was the sudden vision of seeing his career as a graphic designer go down the plughole which frightened Fintan. He "got into a lot of trouble" with the police in Dublin. "I was up in the courthouse the next day. I was terrified. I was terrified of the press getting hold of it, too, because that would be the end of my reputation, my job." Fintan was in a serious relationship at the time, but the young woman was also using. ("Two addicts together is far, far worse. If one of you tries to get clean, the other pulls them back.")

We condemn political figures for "covering up" when a scandal breaks, but quite honestly, when most people get into trouble with the law, the first, self-preservation instinct is to try and effect a "cover up". Fintan managed to keep his court appearance out of the public eye, and he was fortunate to get off with a caution. But the whole episode had the bracing effect of a cold bath. He had been using heroin for eight years, and was extremely dependent, but he had not lost his ambition to be successful at his work.

The entanglement with the law also alerted his mother to the problem.

"My mother was great," Fintan said. How did she cope, I asked?

"She reacted intuitively. She just said — 'What the fuck do you think you are doing? This is a really stupid thing to do. This is a really bad thing to do. You're fucking yourself up'." His parents are educated, progressive people, and divorced: Fintan's mother might have been expected to react like a right-on 60s liberal, anti-authority and "whatever you're into". But no: she "came down on me like a ton of bricks. She gave me both barrels. She wasn't moralistic. It wasn't — 'You've sinned and you'll go to hell'. It was — 'Would you ever cop yourself on.'" She told him, robustly, to get a grip, and face the fact that this would destroy his life and career.

The garda bust probably saved Fintan's life. He began, from that moment, to turn himself around. He didn't get clean straight away: he didn't come off heroin the following week. But he began the journey of trial and error, repeated quitting and relapsing, until, two or three years down the line, he really did get fully clean, and is today committed to a drug-free way of life. His work, incidentally, has greatly benefited from his getting clean. He had to split up with his partner, though they had a child. A recovered addict simply cannot go on living with a using addict, however passionate the attachment.

Alexander, who was living alone at the age of fifteen, and who is now in his thirties, had used and dealt in heroin for about twelve years. He also faced his moment of truth during a police bust. He now sees that during the last four years of his heroin use, "things were going rapidly downhill". He had had some trouble with the police previously, but the final arrest really rattled him. "It was the fact that the whole court case took a year to get through." In the end, the judge was lenient with him — Alexander is a nicely spoken young man, and looked suitably chastised in court. His barrister was also extremely skilful. The judge gave him probation.

But the beak did warn him: "This is your final chance." The charge was intent to supply, which was no more than the truth. Alexander was flagged down by a police car when driving: he was in possession of heroin, which he and his companions tried to disperse by chucking out the window. He was also in possession of £2,500 in cash (he had just spent £1,200, sterling, in cash on buying the heroin which was then dissipated through the night air). He was stopped, as it happened, by the police in Brixton, which is a black neighbourhood. Had he been in Hampstead, he almost certainly would not have aroused police interest. It is a sad paradox that middle-class heroin users, and dealers, are less likely to be stopped by the authorities than poorer people, although the culture shock for middle-class young people may have more impact on their conduct. Poorer people may be more inured to the criminal justice system.

"I took it to heart," Alexander says, of the judge's warning. He was bitterly disillusioned by the reaction of his companions, who were quick to accuse him of "dropping them in it", although he actually took the rap. Junkies themselves say that the heroin world is one of fair-weather friends: solid, close and strong on camaraderie when things are going well. But when the heat is on, quick to cheat on one another, and show disloyalty. His travelling companions were also furious that so much heroin had to be chucked out the window, and to so little avail.

It wasn't just the shock of appearing in court that distressed Alexander. It was the whole palaver leading up to it. It was the meetings with lawyers, the feeling that this eventuality was hanging over him. Somehow, he just "knew" that something was going to have to change. For three years after the event, he went on and off two or three different methadone programmes. This didn't alter his life immediately, either, but it did stop him trading in heroin. "Methadone means you're not dependent on making money in the heroin business." Methadone, too, is traded on the black market: medically prescribed dosages of the replacement drug leak into street use. But you do not have to get involved in criminal activities in order to obtain it in the first place.

Three years after his court case, Alexander made the decision to stop completely. He had a brief relapse, but he got over it.

Two other things also changed in Alexander's life. He decided to go back to university, and he got into college to do a history degree. And he was able to rent some pleasant accommodation in a large house owned by an old friend, who is also an ex-addict. He began to move in circles where people were no longer using. And that is a big, big step.

I remember this well from my drinking days. I felt a sense of sadness and loneliness in leaving behind my pub life and the cronies who had been part of my life. I knew I would have to make new friends, and learn to enjoy human company in sobriety: but the idea just makes you feel forlorn, at first. Yet the funny thing is, addicts sometimes find that they are re-united in a roundabout way with old friends. Clarissa, who took up heroin in Chelsea in her twenties, partly to cope with her own confused and anxious feelings, and partly because she thought her mother's arty friends, who did drugs, were frightfully cool and hip. Now she runs into those of them who have survived at Narcotics Anonymous and Alcoholic Anonymous meetings. And they are a lot better company when clear of drugs.

Those who survive the drug years are almost like survivors of a war. They remember those who did not survive, and think themselves lucky. Maura Russell of the Rutland Clinic in Dublin says — the addict either dies, or gets clean, by their middle or late thirties. There are just a few, very unusual exceptions to this.

Kicking the habit in the thirties is a recognised pattern of heroin use. People get burned out, fed up, and frankly, bored with the interminable round of conniving and scoring. They want to settle down. They want a life. They want a marriage, a relationship: they want to go straight. And just as a group of thirty-somethings will find themselves getting married around the same time, having babies around the same time, so it can also happen that a group of friends will spontaneously quit drugs around the same time. This may not be consciously known to the group: it just "emerges".

This is what occurred in Paul and Jill's circle, in a Yorkshire city. Paul and Jill are in their mid-thirties. They had been doing heroin for the best part of fifteen years. Paul started experimenting with his peers, in 1982 and 1983: within months of starting, everyone in his circle of friends was using it. He introduced Jill to it. Paul got busted in the 1980s, but he was one of those people for whom a season in prison didn't halt his habit. He came from a working-class (and strongly socialist) background where a jail sentence did not carry a huge sense of shame. "My friends just saw it as damned unfortunate ... but he'll be back in a few months."

But the number of deaths they experienced among friends and contemporaries had more of an impact on the couple. "Most of the 'characters' that I knew have gone from the drug scene," Paul reflects: they are dead. Both he and Jilly have come close to death. In 1990, Paul deliberately learned cardio-pulmonary resuscitation, in case he would ever need it. He has needed it. He has saved Jilly's life, four times, when she slipped into respiratory arrest, and her lips began to turn blue. Another friend of theirs, Sharon, is cross-addicted to drink and heroin: he has also saved her several times. "It's always the breathing that goes, with opiates, because the body is so relaxed. You just breathe out, and you don't breathe in again. If you don't deal with it, you've got a dead friend.

Then, recently, Jill's biological clock began to tick, as also happens with women in their thirties. "I realised that everyone around me was starting to get a life, starting to get on with things, and a friend had recently got pregnant. And I thought, that's something that I can't do, or am much less likely to do, because of my habit." The menstrual cycle can disappear, or decline, for women using heroin.

They had also used up a lot of money. Jill had come into an inheritance of £40,000 from a grandfather's building business, and they had blown it all on heroin. The first £20,000 disappeared within three months. They were utterly broke. And so they made the decision to stop, together, using methadone initially. Paul's health was beginning to suffer, too, and he had had a bout of Hepatitis C, a liver infection to which drug users are vulnerable.

Then they discovered that quite coincidentally, four other couples they knew were also deciding to quit. It seemed, almost, as though there were a telepathic collective signal, going around a circle of contemporaries. Paul had started as part of a "peer pressure" movement: he was now quitting with those friends who had survived. It wasn't easy for the couple, as I could see. But they had come to the end of a line with heroin, and they did have a milieu of contemporaries to support them.

Occasionally, a religious experience will help; or more likely, a "spiritual experience".

Margaret, for example, was sitting on a bar-stool planning her own suicide.

After years of abusing a cocktail of drugs, she decided that the only way she could really control her life was by killing herself. In the middle of this strategic plan, she felt as though an invisible hand reached out to her and touched her. It was, to her, a palpable experience of a "higher power" which literally saved her life. Her recovery began at that very moment.

Addicts often have an aversion to any kind of organised religion, which they will regard as part of a repressive authoritarian structure. It is also part of their general nihilism — "there is no meaning to life, so who cares?" In Ireland, addicts are often bitterly anti-Catholic, and will repulse any suggestion of church support. "I have no time for the Catholic Church," says Margaret. Why? "Because I saw no love in it." When she started her recovery, she began going to Narcotics Anonymous meetings, but refused to attend Alcoholic Anonymous meetings (which can equally help drug users), because in Ireland the Lord's Prayer is usually recited at AA meetings. "So sectarian," she condemned.

Yet, when visiting the United States, she was happy to join in Native American prayers when attending AA meetings especially convened for the Sioux people. She perceived, with a rueful smile, the double standard that was being applied — Christian prayers disbarred, Native American prayers embraced. But her attitude is, I think, characteristic of contempt for the Church among what I might call the drug classes. Thomas, a Dubliner with a serious HIV condition, who hailed from the inner-city part of old Dublin, where once the flickering light to the Sacred Heart burned brightly in every tenement room, was completely dismissive of the Church. "The biggest Mafia in the world," he said contemptuously. "The Vatican launders the Mafia's money, anyway. I never did get on with the priests. I knew people that were interfered with."

Fintan made a very strong distinction between spirituality and the organised churches. He, too, would have no truck with churches. "I would have been very anti-religion — any religion." It was only after being involved with Narcotics Anonymous that he began to open up towards spirituality. "The whole spiritual side to the NA programme is something that I try very hard to engage with. And I respect it, hugely. The Buddhist sense of it, especially. It doesn't offend me. But Catholicism would be a different kettle of fish for me. A lot of people I would meet have been abused by the Catholic Church, literally. Physically, sexually, emotionally, mentally. When they look up at the wall and see 'We ask God to remove our shortcomings', they often have a very violent reaction to it. And it takes quite a while to realise that that is not necessarily equated with Catholicism, you know." After a substantial period living clean, the addict may sometimes return to a church; following your own road to spirituality can sometimes seem like reinventing the wheel.

Recovering addicts will often become more open to some form of spirituality, when they see it helping people. Besides, Fintan says, "Addiction is an inverted spirituality. Spirituality is becoming aware ... it's humility, becoming aware of one's place in the world, neither greater nor less than other people. Addiction is the direct opposite of that: it's being so self-centred and self-absorbed it's not possible to think of others. So it's impossible to be religious or spiritual and be an active addict. It's anti-spirituality."

Addicts often talk about how their moral selves became eroded by the drug: it is not that you want to become selfish, or uncaring to others. It is not that you don't love those around you; but heroin eats up everything inside your moral self. It is absolutely pointless for family members to say — "Give it up for our sake." I have never heard of an addict successfully quitting because a family member says — "Please give it up for our sake" or "Don't do this to me". The addict may love someone else dearly, but he can only make a change for himself. The book that Marsha Hunt has edited — *The Junk Yard* — in which imprisoned addicts speak about their own lives, shows how deeply heroin users can love their families. When all else is gone, the attachment to parents, wives, children will remain — particularly, indeed, to children. But though the family members may be able to encourage at the right moment, no addict seems to be make the decision to quit, effectively, for anyone else's sake.

It seems to have to be something that happens to them, personally. Ben, the art teacher in his twenties, made the decision to quit after a particularly traumatic session in which he was horrified by his own actions. "Seen *Trainspotting*?" he refers to the film of the Irving Welsh book. "OK. Get rid of all the atmospheric lights. Get rid of all the beautiful, wonderful characters. Get rid of all that. That's exactly how I was. Sitting there, in all that squalor."

His need for heroin grew with the habit of taking it, as it so often does. "I needed heroin so much that I injected a woman in her neck — because she needed a hit, and I needed some of her smack." The jugular vein is a known site for injecting; as is the groin; as is the eyeball. Addicts will use all three, if desperate.

"I needed it so much. I needed heroin so much that I injected a woman into her neck. I sat there and did it. She would deal out my heroin. I sit there injecting into her neck, and a ten year old boy walks in, and he's got no clothes on, because somebody has stolen his clothes to sell them for junk. A ten year old kid, man. It was her child. Her own kid. He seemed such a bright little kid. I bought him some chips ... played football with him. But it was not on. I sat there and let it go by. I went on injecting her. I shouldn't have done. There's no excuse. I knew what was going on. You don't expose children to this sort of stuff, but I know I did it ... What sort of arsehole does that? What sort of arsehole?" He felt a wave of self-disgust after this episode, and went cold turkey, sweating it out with physical pain, frightened, cold, raw, crying for a week without stopping.

And yet, for all he has been through, and for all his insight, Ben remains ambivalent. "I'm not in a sense fully recovered. I'm quite happy to do it again. In spite of everything. You see, it's such an incredible feeling. It's indescribable. Everything that was ever wrong is just gone. You are cleansed. All your anxieties are gone." Although at the time of our interview, Ben was moving towards getting clean, the possibility of relapse remained, I felt. But that happens: a relapse doesn't mean that you won't get clean again. If the hope is there, the recovery will one day be achieved. Each effort to quit is another step forward.

But for some people, the hope becomes extinguished, and they cannot quit heroin. Or they cannot quit heroin for the foreseeable future. Or they quit, and they find life unbearable. This was the case with Brian Gaffney, aged twenty-nine, who died a year after coming off the drug.

Brian was among the very early heroin addicts in Dublin: he started in the 1970s, before the big inrush of cheaper heroin from Iran and Afghanistan onto Western markets. He was, by all accounts, the typical heroin type: that is, with a very pleasing personality, charming, cherished, and "always a gentleman", as his mother Mary puts it.

Mary Gaffney, a petite blonde, now aged sixty-five, lives in a neat house in Tallaght, West Dublin. She has worked in the hotel and catering business all her adult life, as a waitress, and worked hard to keep her family. She had three sons, and one daughter. Her children grew up, and after some initial problems, settled down, and did well; her youngest son, Raymond, is a university graduate and a senior manager with Pepsi Cola in the United States. She has a grand-daughter at Loreto College in Dublin, now one of the best girls' schools in

Dublin, and, as it happens, my own alma mater. She is hugely proud of her grandson, Patrick, who is a steady boy with a good job as a printer.

But Mary's second son, Brian, adorable and adored, was one of those lads who would try anything. I identify: I would have tried anything myself, as a teenager, and was only fortunate that I did not get the chance to try drugs. At twelve, Brian tried barbiturates. He was expelled from school, a technical school in Inchicore, though the headmaster told his mother that the lad had "brains to burn". But he was clearly disruptive at school (in rather the same manner as I was, by the way). Then, at that dangerous, dangerous age of fifteen, he fell in with "the wrong crowd": that is, a known family of drug criminals in Dublin, whose main area for trafficking drugs was the charming old square of St Stephen's Green. Brian was used as a "runner", and was soon using heroin himself.

The course of events broke his mother's heart. Mary, who was a widow at forty-four (although she had already left her husband, who was a moody, difficult, controlling man, "with no compassion", before he died from a heart attack) did everything she could to help Brian. She supported him when he went into one of the first Irish clinics for addicts, Coolmine, and supported him when he came out. He was de-toxed three or four times there. He turned to criminal activities — mostly passing dud cheques — to support his habit, which back in the 1970s and 80s, required £600-£700 a day. (Heroin was a lot more expensive at that period, than it became in the 1990s.) Working as a waitress herself, Mary once had to pay £400 to a drug-dealer whom Brian owed: she worked for that money, on her feet, and paid it. The drug dealers had already broken Brian's legs once, for non-payment.

Brian injected everywhere. "He got that he had no veins left. He was injecting in his penis." But then a final detox did get him off heroin, and for the best part of a year, he stayed off it too. He was a good reader, and he read a lot during his last year. He went walking. The main thing was, he stayed away from town, from the centre of Dublin city where all the temptation lay.

But in 1985, Brian killed himself with an overdose of tablets, which he had carefully saved up. His mother believes that the craving for heroin had come back, but he had lost his nerve: "he no longer had the bottle go out and do what he would have to do to get it.

"Brian went out of this world to get away from heroin," Mary says. "The habit was too strong. He hated himself for being a heroin addict." And yet he couldn't live without it. He left a note for his mother which said: "Ma, I sorry for the way things have turned out ...You know I love you, but I am just fed up living. Goodbye and take care of yourself. I love you, Brian."

About six months after his death, Mary had a vivid dream in which Brian came to her. "He was very blond as a child. He appeared to me as if he was ten years old. All blond and a lovely body — later he had tattoos. And I said to him, 'Brian, what are you doing with yourself?' And he said, 'Ma, don't worry about me. I'm an angel now.'"

William Burroughs observes that "Suicide is frequent among ex-junkies." This is something which crops up anecdotally: all recovering addicts know people who have committed suicide a year, two years, after quitting heroin. Rehab clinic directors all refer to patients whom they considered a real success. "He was doing so well, clean for three, five years. And then I got a call that a suicide had occurred." It is as though life was afterwards too flat. They couldn't live with heroin and couldn't live without it. The alarming increase in suicide rates in Ireland during the 1990s almost certainly includes cases of addicts who got clean, but their lives, and their sense of hope, had been too destroyed by heroin to ever truly recover.

Yet it doesn't have to be that way. There can always be hope, while there is life.

How to help an addict –
by a recovering addict.

Let them know you know.

Don't hide it.

Let them know you care.

But do not enable.

Say: "I know what's going on."

Give them the books and the literature.

Show them where they can get help.

But hardly ever can you *force* someone to get well.

Don't enable: but support.

Be open. Refer as openly to heroin as you might to a glass of wine.

Don't nag or reprimand. But don't approve or collaborate.

Don't throw them out of home immediately. But if you have to save the rest of the family, you may have to ask them to go.

Sometimes there is a moment when they are ready.

There was someone who tried to get clean for sixteen years: and after sixteen years, the moment came. She did it.

Spirituality can help. But it is not available to everyone.

If they aren't ready, they aren't ready.

If they aren't ready, maybe they have to go back out there until they are ready.

Maybe they'll die before they are ready.

Accept that this is a risk you take.

Accept that when you have done your best, there is nothing more you can do.

131

Nobody believes addiction is going to happen to them.

Everyone thinks at first they can control it.

The drug always ends up controlling the person.

Understand their powerlessness.

Be kind: suggest new options in life.

Let them know you know. Let them know you care.

Be open. Be strong. Do not cover up for them.

Do not tell lies for them, phoning in with false excuses
   for missed appointments.

Love them, respect them, but do not enable.

*With thanks to Margaret, a kind veteran of Narcotics
Anonymous.*

Chapter Seven

Methods of Recovery

I know people who have benefited from every type of treatment there is.
— Michael Audreson, clinic director.

Try everything. Every intervention has a chance to succeed.
— Maura Russell, clinic director.

There are many different treatments for heroin addiction; and different people will benefit from different approaches.

Different approaches will also continue to develop in the future. If we consider that heroin only became a serious social problem in the 1970s and 1980s, even by the end of the century we are still at an early phase of understanding and remedy. Attitudes to the treatment of the heroin addict altered a lot over the last forty years of the twentieth century, and will no doubt alter again. In the 1960s, psychotherapy was thought to provide the answer, and psychotherapy with a strong father-figure. "Because of his personality defects," wrote H. Dale Beckett of the Royal College of Psychiatrists, in 1967, "an addict needs a strong, stable one-to-one relationship with a wise male adult who will be able to play the role of a deficient father."

Until recently (and still, in some unenlightened quarters), the heroin addict is simply regarded as a criminal, whose disappearance would be a small loss to society. When Mary Gaffney's son, Brian, went for treatment in Dublin in the early 1980s, Mary found the doctors supercilious and dismissive. One said to her, callously — "These junkies usually end up killing themselves." His attitude seemed to be that it was both inevitable and insignificant. Despite the doctor's authority, and Mary's modest social position, she retorted: "Excuse me, that's my son you're talking about, out there. He's not a piece of meat."

Mary came to realise that, indeed, many heroin addicts whom Brian knew, did die young. But she still felt, and rightly, that even a junkie deserves respect. The Merchants Quay project in Dublin, founded in 1989 by a Franciscan priest, Sean Cassin, was based on this approach: that the heroin user is a person and must be respected. The heroin user may think very lowly of himself, particularly when he is trying to get off the drug. The last thing he needs is contempt. The first item on the prescription list should be hope.

When Brian Gaffney was being treated at a clinic, Mary was told that she must throw him out of the house, and not give him shelter. She objected to this, too. She could not turn away her own son. The clinic's regulation was an approach of "tough love" which has since modified. There are fewer hard and fast rules of advice given now. "Sometimes it's impossible to say which is right," says Maura Russell of the Rutland Clinic in Dublin, which several recoverers praised to me. "I would not advise parents to put them out of home. Because it's a very big decision to make. If things go wrong, you might feel, if we hadn't been advised to put him out of home, this wouldn't have happened. But sometimes the decision to keep them at home results in their deaths.

"With any intervention, you have no idea whether it is going to work or not. When there is a tragedy, every single family asks: 'Could we have done more? Did we handle it wrongly? Could we have done it different?' There really is no answer to this."

The simplest way to come off heroin is just to stop: to go "cold turkey", or as it is now called, "clucking". It is a very uncomfortable experience, and the body is in a shaking, painful condition for days. The body is more vulnerable to pain: the loss of the opiate has already altered the chemistry of the nervous system. "The addict gets a pain and the body says, there'll be a bit of heroin along in a minute," says Pauline Bissett, the Chief Executive of Broadway Lodge, in Somerset. So it doesn't do its own job. Other "normal" pains can seem much more acute in recovery — arthritis, headaches. Heroin is, after all, a brilliant painkiller. The removal of heroin also unmasks medical problems that had been untreated. "A patient was admitted with a very large hole in his foot which he was completely unaware of. He had medicated himself so much [with heroin] that he didn't notice."

Descriptions of the "cold turkey" process are vividly painful in themselves. "I felt physical pain for a week," says Ben. "I remember travelling on a bus, yeah, and getting spontaneous ejaculation because of the vibration of the bus. The hold it has over your body —- the fluids are just running out, everywhere. Disgusting. Your nose is running. You're crying — the slightest thing will set you off. It's not just the physical stuff, either. It's all the other emotional stuff that you've covered up, flowing out of you." In her autobiographical book about being a heroin addict, Tam Stewart says that each "cold turkey" experience may be slightly different, because much depends upon the amount of drugs used and the length of time using. But it is never agreeable and it can be a torment: aching, depressing, emotional, sweat-drenched, stomach-churning, bowel-loosening and sleepless, lasting generally about four days. It is sometimes compared to a dose of flu, but it can feel a lot worse.

But medics also underline the fact that no one has ever died from the physical consequences of quitting heroin. "People do not die of heroin withdrawal," says Dr Bill Shanahan, an opiate expert at the Chelsea and Westminster Hospital in London. "Ever. It's flu-like at the worst. It's unpleasant. And frankly, half of it is psychological."

The psychological aspect of heroin withdrawal is borne out by this interesting test. When admitted to a detox clinic, patients are assessed, and the process of detoxification is commenced. The patient usually dreads this process, as he has heard, on the grapevine, how anguishing it is. The amount he suffers, however, will often depend on how the peer group around him is responding, or how well the person just ahead of him is responding. If a person has a very low threshold of pain — and men tend to feel pain sooner than women — and he goes through a bad time, then the person after him will also feel he is going through a bad time. But a patient who does well will often have a "contagion effect" on the one who follows.

Some addicts will go through a "cold turkey" on their own; it is done, it has been done and it can be done. But as I have been told, over and over again, it's not getting off the drug that is the hardest part: it is staying off. A motivated addict could go from self-administered cold turkey to Narcotics Anonymous meetings (or attend

Alcoholics Anonymous if there is not an NA meeting in the area). But it is a tremendous struggle, and self-cure in this way has a high element of relapse. Addicts are not, in general, advised to tackle the anguish of withdrawal on their own. A period of "stabilising" the heroin addict with the accepted replacement drug, methadone, is usually advised. In fact, methadone maintenance is now the most widely used method in the world of healing heroin addiction.

Methadone is a synthetic narcotic and analgesic — a medical word for pain-reliever — invented in Germany just before the Second World War. A leading American encyclopaedia on drugs claims that its first brand name "Dolphine", was so called as a tribute to Adolf Hitler, but it is also said to be derived from "dolor", the Latin word for grief. Methadone has similar effects to morphine and heroin, and produces some of the same euphoria, and drowsiness; but it does not slow down the respiration, as heroin will do. Its effects also last longer than heroin. A heroin users may inject four times a day; with methadone, it need only be taken once (usually orally, though it can be injected. Some addicts are actually addicted to injections.)

The Methadone Maintenance programme in the treatment of heroin was developed by two American doctors, Vincent Dole and Marie Nyswander in 1967, and American research has consistently supported its use. Many medical papers continue to regard Methadone Maintenance as a highly effective treatment, showing successful outcomes in tests. It was particularly effective in treating American soldiers who had become addicted to heroin during the Vietnam war. Within a year, over eighty per cent of these Vietnam vets were clean of heroin use, as a result of a Methadone Maintenance treatment.

However, the Vietnam veterans who had become heroin addicts were not necessarily a representative sample of heroin users, as exist today. Society changes, and those using heroin today are different people, and different groups of people, from heroin users of the 1960s and 70s. Soldiers in Vietnam took heroin as a psychological shield against the experiences of that odious war. On returning home, most of them were keen, and motivated, to get back to normal life. They were, as a group, different from the heroin addict of civil society today, who will be someone who has chosen the habit and opiate way of life, or has been drawn into heroin use because of a personal, or perhaps chemical, vulnerability.

Nevertheless, methadone, sometimes called by its trade name, Physeptone, is, in Ireland and Britain, the most common form of treatment for a heroin addict who has sought treatment for his addiction. The bottle of Physeptone, disbursed either through the general practitioner, or through a local or community based clinic, is the standard treatment. In seeking to tackle the heroin problem — or at least, in being seen by the voters to "do something" — politicians promise more Methadone Maintenance clinics. And this is widely supported by medical opinion, and by users in search of a cure. Heroin addicts in Dublin complain that not enough Methadone Maintenance clinics are available to them, and there is thus generally a waiting list for treatment.

In the Irish system, the addict is prescribed methadone "for as long as they need it". This could be, in the words of one doctor working in a community clinic, from one to ten years, providing that the addict is otherwise clean (of heroin) and stable. His urine must be monitored regularly to check that he is not using heroin as well.

Methadone Maintenance undoubtedly can help bring the addict through a difficult bridging period from heroin use to the ultimate goal of abstinence. It is seen as a useful tool, both social and personal, of "harm reduction." But it is far from being a cure-all. Addicts may simply switch their addiction from heroin to methadone, which some critics regard as about as useful as an alcoholic switching his liquor intake from whiskey to gin. Or, during periods when it is not possible to monitor their urine, they merely add it to their general cocktail. Methadone has its uses, clearly, but it is nevertheless replacing one drug habit with another.

Yet when an addict is quitting a serious drug habit, he has to replace his drug with something. When I first got sober, I went to the cinema obsessively, as well as to 12-step meetings. The fantasy world of drinking was replaced by the fantasy story-telling world of the movies. So what? Going to the cinema never did anyone any harm. Marek Kohn, in his interesting book "Narcomania" says that the trouble with self-help groups like AA and NA is that addicts then become addicted to going to meetings. So what, again? No one ever died from going to too many meetings, either.

But there are some very serious criticisms of Methadone Maintainence. And some of these suggest that methadone is not just a harmless replacement — it can be just as harmful as heroin. In a research paper published in 1999, it was found that in one sample seventy per cent of addicts receiving methadone treatment had also used heroin over a three-month period. Sometimes the methadone dose seemed insufficient, and the user "topped up" with what he still felt was this "real thing". If prescription levels of methadone are low, the addict may be more likely to "top up" with the real thing.

Sometimes methadone simply endorsed the idea that using a drug was a normal way of life.

And medically prescribed methadone leaks into the black and grey markets. I have met former heroin addicts, now using methadone as a replacement drug, who manage to collect two or three prescriptions of methadone a day, selling on part of it for street use. (When doctors are prudent to prescribe low dosages, the user will find several sources.)

As a drug, methadone is just as dangerous as heroin, when abused. In a well-researched, but alarming study that Raymond Byrne has written as a thesis, he demonstrates that the mortality rate of methadone, in Dublin, is twice that of heroin itself. "In Dublin in 1998, people who took methadone were apparently at least twice as likely to have methadone implicated in their deaths as those who took heroin (alone) would have heroin implicated in their deaths." Since October 1998 a new "Methadone Protocol" has been introduced by the Eastern Health Board in Dublin which is designed to tighten controls of methadone prescription, though this does not invalidate Mr Byrne's findings, which demonstrate the danger of the drug.

"Methadone," comments Dr Adrian Garfoot, of the Laybourne Clinic in the East End of London, "is an evil drug." Dr Garfoot has treated over 800 heroin addicts in his practice and he sees the methadone route being routinely abused. Many radical doctors wonder if Methadone Maintenance isn't simply a political, rather than an actual, remedy. If it isn't just another American-led strategy to combat a "war on drugs" which can never really be won by prohibition.

There is a growing anti-methadone lobby among grass-roots recoverers. Kerry Condron of Glasgow, a recovered addict herself, has been vociferous in the British media in her criticism of Methadone Maintenance. Methadone, she says, is harder to kick, and kills more people. I have a lot of empathy with this viewpoint: my nephew Patrick died from methadone, mixed with alcohol and topped up with heroin. It is possible that had he stayed using heroin alone until he was genuinely ready to quit opiates, he might still be alive. He was prescribed methadone over a Christmas holiday period, which meant that he would not be tested for urine over several days. His methadone intake was relatively low — 40 milligrams on the morning of the day he died — but enough to spell fatality when mixed with heroin and wine. PK would number among Raymond Byrne's statistics of those who died having both methadone and heroin in their systems, this being a higher toll than those using heroin as the only opiate.

I came to feel that while Methadone Maintenance might work in very carefully controlled and monitored circumstances, it is no remedy in itself. It can be a helping agent, but it should be warily regarded, and methadone policy should be constantly reviewed.

Rehabilitation clinics, where the patient goes to stay for several weeks at a time, use methadone in conjunction with other therapies, and as a limited, bridging medication.

Let me describe the way that methadone is used at Broadway Lodge in Weston-super-Mare, Somerset, as an example of strictly limited application.

"The patients arrive here in the morning, usually having used a bit," says Pauline Bissett, whose background is in nursing and medical care. "We know they are usually going to have used [heroin]. We take the temperature, pulse and blood pressure. When a patient starts to go into withdrawal, the blood pressure will rise — usually it's very low at the start. It will then start to go up. We would have a rise of fifteen points in blood pressure.

"The amount of methadone we would give would correspond to the amount of heroin — sort of. We have to test carefully: we cannot go completely on what they are telling us. We will convert what they are using into the methadone equivalent.

"Seventy milligrams is, however, the maximum we would give.

"Having converted what they are using, we may up it a bit, and we divide the methadone into four doses, which they get each day. We are keeping up with the withdrawal symptoms, but we are not giving it to them in one dose so that they get the rush.

"From a ceiling of 70 milligrams a days, we drop by 10 milligrams daily until total daily use is 40 milligrams. Then we drop by 5 milligrams daily until the total daily is 20 milligrams. Then we drop by two and a half milligrams daily until they are completely off. The doses are divided throughout the day. This should take ten days to two weeks. They generally feel OK.

"This is the procedure we have refined over fifteen years. We used to do it much more quickly. They used to have some diarrhoea. But dropping by half towards the end is better. Right at the end of their detox we give them 25 milligrams of librium, just to help them kick-start their

sleeping patterns, for four days after they finish their detox. After that, it's abstinence. And re-education."

The twelve-step programme, as pioneered by
Alcoholics Anonymous, and taken up by others, as in the
Minnesota Method, is regarded as "unbeatable", at
Broadway Lodge. Moreover, it is absolutely recognised
that recovering addicts have to have "something else in
their lives" if they are not to relapse. "You can detox
patients over and over again, but if they don't have
anything else in their lives, they are going to relapse,"
says Pauline Bissett. "You can detox people over and over
again, but if you don't teach them another way to deal
with what life flings at them, they are going to pick up a
chemical substance again."

There are many variations on this approach
throughout the growing number of detox clinics
throughout Britain and Ireland. As in all fields of
endeavour, one specialist may be critical of another's:
drug treatment is such a huge speciality now there are
bound to be many differences, and some people with the
means to do so will "shop around" for the approach that
suits them.

At one famous clinic in Wiltshire, the detox drug
clonidine is used in the course of detoxification. Others
favour Lofexidine, in conjunction with a benzodiazepam.
One recovering addict raged at the over-use of these
prescription drugs: "These guys are just pill-pushers."

"Detoxing is the easy bit, especially with modern
techniques," says Dr Colin Brewer, who has a clinic in
Belgravia, London, and uses techniques still considered
unusual in Britain. And then he reiterates the point that
everyone has made: "It's staying clean that's tricky,
especially if the patient/user/abuser doesn't really want

to stop just yet. As a general rule, people around thirty, who are often growing out of heroin, are much easier to treat than people around twenty, who are often just getting into their pharmacological stride. Someone with a short history — only using regularly for a year or two - employed or employable, with support from friends or family and who has other hobbies as well as taking drugs, should be encouraged to try getting opiate-free."

Dr Brewer is an advocate of a medical drug called Naltrexone, a narcotic antagonist popular in the treatment of heroin addicts in Spain and Israel. (It is also now being hailed as a new miracle treatment for alcohol abuse, at the current cost of about £3,000 sterling a year.) "The opiate receptor blockade is so effective that for practical purposes it cannot be overcome even by four or five times the average daily heroin dose of most addicts," he has written in a research paper on the treatment. "It is the only treatment for heroin abuse for which it is possible to give patients a virtual guarantee that if they take it regularly in the prescribed dose, they cannot become re-addicted to heroin." It works rather as Antabuse (disulfiram) works against alcohol: as an antagonist in the body. If you drink alcohol while you are on Antabuse you feel very ill indeed: I have tried it, and it felt as though I was having a seizure. The alcoholic will often deal with this problem of nausea and panic by leaving off the Antabuse and taking up with the alcohol again, and the same pattern obtains with Naltrexone: the addict needs to be supervised.

In a study cited by Dr Brewer, Naltrexone proved to be effective as a condition of probation by offenders: but supervision was essential to its success.

Naltrexone is thus suggested as an alternative treatment to Methadone: it can be given orally, or as an implant. It can be administered as a general anaesthesia, or what the French call a "sleep cure". "Detoxing under anaesthesia or sedation can give you 100% success in that phase of treatment and naltrexone implants will give virtually 100% abstinence rates for the first four to six weeks," Dr Brewer says. "The longer people stay clean after detox, the longer they're likely to stay clean, especially if they stay clean in the real world and not in the artificial world of the clinic.

"Most people can resist temptation if they're immured in a big country house with a lousy bus service; the test is to keep on resisting it back home when people come knocking on your door and your life is still far from satisfying." Seeing old friends who are still using is what the Catholic Church used to call "an occasion of sin": a real source of temptation.

"Naltrexone — whether implanted or taken under rigorous family supervision — makes relapse in this vulnerable phase much more difficult. Naltrexone stops you from reverting to heroin and forces you to learn or relearn alternative habits until they become automatic. (Hazlitt: 'We do nothing well until we do it without thinking about it.')

"Counselling" — as opposed to support and encouragement — is an overrated activity. For most people, the evidence suggests that regular naltrexone with minimal counselling is more effective than regular counselling with minimal naltrexone. Naturally, this is a highly unpopular view within the counselling industry. The answer to the statement: "I want counselling [or I want my son to have it] so that I can find out why I took heroin" is generally: "You took it for the same reasons that you tried cigarettes, alcohol, and wearing the clothes that your peer-group wear, and the same reasons that make other people take up hang-gliding, rock-climbing and other exciting but dangerous activities. It is learned behaviour and up to a point, you can unlearn it if you want to."

Dr Brewer's views — and some of his medical approaches — are regarded as controversial by some in the competitive business of helping heroin addicts. But if different approaches work for different people, we need to know what all these are.

Dr Bill Shanahan's views on treating heroin addicts are equally controversial. Dr Shanahan is experienced in his field, running a local authority clinic in West London, practising at the Chelsea and Westminster Hospital, and being involved also at the private Charter Nightingale rehabilitation clinic, near Regents Park. As it happens, he is Irish, though his work with addicts has been in London.

Dr Shanahan actually believes that one of the best ways in which chronic heroin addicts might be treated is by giving them — under proper medical supervision — heroin. Pharmaceutical heroin (diamorphine) costs the National Health Service £1.12 pence an ampoule: rather less than the equivalent cost of street heroin at £10 a shot (though the street price, like any other market commodity, varies). And, obviously it is an awful lot less dangerous than street heroin.

Britain is one of the few countries in which heroin can be legally prescribed (although under very restrictive Government licence. There are about fifty active prescribers). Doctors can find it difficult to get Home Office licences to prescribe — conferences on heroin addiction are told of doctors being repeatedly refused this amenity. So prescribing remains rare; methadone accounts for 96 per cent of all opiate prescriptions for treating drug dependency, in the UK.

In a trial carried out in Dr Shanahan's West London treatment clinic, fifty-six eligible patients were recruited for a study on treatment using both methadone and diamorphine, the medical form of heroin. Their median age was thirty-eight, and they had been injecting heroin, on average, for nineteen years. They had all had several previous attempts to come off heroin, without success.

Thirty-seven of the group chose to receive diamorphine (heroin) under medical supervision. Three months later, the patients were doing well, they had considerably reduced their use of street drugs, they were healthier, and less prone to crime. There were significant improvements in employment, housing and relation-ships. Between six and twelve months later, there was also significant reductions in HIV risk behaviour and in sexual risk behaviour.

The research paper written by Dr Shanahan and three other colleagues concluded that for long-term users of heroin, those who had tried all other treatments and failed, the option of giving them what they were addicted to, in safe conditions, and with provisions that they would not abuse or sell on their prescriptions (empty ampoules had to be returned, like empty milk bottles), was helpful and constructive. There are some individuals who just cannot quit heroin, or cannot quit using it yet. It seems to me a perfectly reasonable proposal that some specialised doctors should be able to prescribe diamorphine for such a group, in very carefully controlled circumstances.

"If we could safely give people heroin to the level they wanted, we could pull in all those street users, using unsafe, impure, uncertain levels of drugs, so that they would not overdose," says Dr Shanahan. "We have intelligent, bright addicts saying to us, we don't care what your policies are. We want heroin and we are going to go and get it, whether you think we should or not.

"If I give them drugs, under proper medical supervision, they won't die. They won't steal." And eventually, Dr Shanahan says, they will "burn out" their heroin use, without killing themselves and turning to crime in the meantime.

There could be considerable opposition to the idea that heroin addicts should be facilitated by a health service. Some anti-drug campaigners are opposed to the needle exchange system now practised routinely (whereby addicts exchange old needles for new, to avoid HIV and hepatitis). They call that "enabling". But in very hard cases, where a heroin user is likely to die from street use, or from heroin-and-methadone cocktails, it is surely worth considering.

Prescribing heroin medically has also been done in Switzerland, and three cities in Germany are exploring methods of allowing chronic heroin users to use heroin safely. This is also happening in Australia.

The first clinical trial in Switzerland, of prescribing heroin to chronic, long-term heroin addicts, began in 1994 and ended in 1996: it reduced by half the number of drug-related deaths in Switzerland. Deaths from AIDS-related illness also began to fall substantially from 1994. (Previously, the Swiss had had a celebrated, or notorious, "needle-park" in Zurich, an area in which heroin users were free to use, without supervision. It was a social disaster, and created a heroin slum: it also acted as a direct enabler to heroin users.)

A programme of medicalised heroin administration continues in Switzerland. The Swiss claim that it has proved to be beneficial, under the strict conditions operating: that the user has failed at least twice in conventional treatment, that there are obvious signs of physical or psychological disorder or neglect, that there is no likely chance of rehabilitation through other forms of treatment and that they are at least twenty years of age. They must also have been using heroin for at least two years. The Swiss programme is about "harm reduction", and that means in the interest of society as to that of the individual. It is about reduction in street crime, muggings and delinquency, as well as personal health and well-being.

There are objections raised to this Swiss approach. One, from abstinence-based activists who feel that the official administration of heroin is an endorsement of the heroin habit. The only long-term cure really *is* abstinence. Thus there are doctors and drug treatment experts in Switzerland itself who are critical of the injection programmes. The other objection, from the opposite end of the spectrum, is from libertarians who regard state injection practice as a form of "State control" and "policing of individuals". They dislike the intense amount of "supervision" and control involved. They call it "pharmacological Calvinism" — regulating heroin as a State medicine, in disciplined conditions, and above all, in contradistinction to any suggestion of pleasure. The Swiss heroin addict is obliged to take his injection under the eye of a supervisory nurse, who may not be directly disapproving, but is seldom overjoyed by the regular sight of a chronic junkie shooting up.

In Germany, there is, similarly, a facility called "injecting rooms", in some cities. Federal law towards heroin is repressive, but an official "blind eye" has been turned towards city policy in Frankfurt, Bremen and Hamburg, where health officials have provided special rooms for chronic heroin addicts. The rooms are bare and clinical, but spotlessly clean and well-maintained. The user is provided with a clean set of "works" as he enters and signs: syringe, ampoule of heroin, and swab all laid out neatly in a kidney dish. The user enters the room, takes possession of his allocated works, and injects his heroin. There is something almost surrealistically clinical about the setting and procedure (and the neighbourhood where the injecting rooms are placed is not too thrilled to have them there), but deaths by overdose in the cities involved have reduced. That fact alone seems to me to make the experiment worthwhile.

An illustrated lecture about the injecting rooms in Germany was shown at a conference in London on heroin in July 1999. After the address a drugs community worker from south London — by all appearances a radical feminist — commented irately, to the German lecturer: "I'll let you watch my clients shoot up heroin when you let me watch you fuck."

These are controversial areas, and there needs to be a lot more debate about harm reduction policies generally.

In Ireland, Dr John O'Connor of the National Drugs Treatment Centre says that what may be effective in Switzerland would not necessarily work in Ireland. These are different societies. This is fair comment: you have to make allowance for cultural differences and diversity. Neither the Irish nor the English are as well-ordered in social responses as some of the Continental peoples. But we still have to go on looking at what works, at what saves lives, and at what gives hope for freedom from the deathly spectre of heroin.

Memo from Jill:
"We don't support the family enough."

Jill is a widow living on the south coast of England. She has two sons; the eldest is a "high flyer" and graduated from Cambridge University. The younger , now aged twenty-seven, became involved with drugs at Edinburgh University. After eight years struggling with a cocktail of opiates and pills, he is "more stable" but living one day at a time. But he finds it hard to cope with life, haunted by feelings of inadequacy and despair, which drug use had blocked off. Jill knows that some individuals are subject to these anxieties; but she feels that the "new world order" − globalised capitalism , the consumer society − has greatly added to the pressures on vulnerable and sensitive young people.

Of course, behind the generality of the drug addiction lies each person's life history and problems, which they have tried to come to terms with through drug taking. Certainly boys without fathers find coping with the adult world especially difficult, and I know two cases where the boys in question turned to the dubious comfort of drugs to provide themselves with the feelings of 'security' and 'protection' a father would normally give.

But I still feel that the family has to be strengthened, parents properly informed and their influence and instruction to their children endorsed by society, and not undermined by insidious laws, agony aunts and psychological gurus. Young people need to be protected for as long as possible so that when the storms of life hit, as they do sooner or later, they have the necessary balance and strength to deal with them. I have recently spent a holiday with a French family in Brittany, and it was wonderful to see the way this well-ordered family helped and supported the young. They all had their meals together, and yes, they accepted the father's authority, which wasn't tyrannical, but it was firm. All this gives the young people a structure when they make their own way in the world.

The world young people go into now is in some ways barbaric. The whole thing is run on money. It is a frighteningly competitive jungle; and then we are told, in any case, that we are just animals at the top of the animal chain. Man's greatest works of creation have been when he believed in something greater than himself. The stresses that young people face, in a society where the family has fragmented and the higher values always seem to be under attack, are almost unbearable, especially for the highly intelligent and sensitive types of young people who take refuge in drugs."

Yours sincerely,

Jill.

Chapter Eight

Growing up in Dublin today
Michelle's Story

Michelle is aged twenty-one, a slim girl with a fine-boned face and neat, straight blonde hair. She grew up in the Clondalkin area of West Dublin, one of six children. There were no special problems in her home: her parents' marriage is stable, and there has never either been violence or unemployment. There is no history of addiction in the family. But like all her friends, Michelle experimented with a range of drugs, from a young age, until she found her "drug of choice" — heroin. She used heroin solidly for four years, and finished up physically and emotionally broken by it. Her adolescenct experiences are not untypical of growing up in city life today.

*

'I have three older sisters, and they are totally, like, perfectly children. I think they just grew up in a different time than I did.

I smoked when I was nine. Cigarettes. I didn't inhale for about a year, but that would have been, like, I loved it. I hung out with girls that were older than me. But even before I picked up anything like that, when I was growing up, Mary, I did not feel normal in myself. I don't even like using the term different. I felt strange. I felt

153

strange in myself. I didn't like myself. I was always looking for approval from other people.

I was a very insecure child. I clinged on to my mother, totally, from a very young age. I don't know what it was — I was the first baby after five years. There was a big gap between me and my sister Jacqueline. But I always felt that they always wanted boys. My mother kept on having kids all the time, to have a boy. There's only a year and a half between me and Martin, who was born after me.

I would have felt very pushed aside. This was the boy. Martin, they called him after me father. And then me mother got pregnant again and a year and a half later, she had Robert. I was just in the middle the whole time. I'm not blaming anyone. It's nothing like that but the way I felt, growing up, it was strange.

My sister told me (when I got clean) that when I was younger I used to try and come in to play with them. The three of them would have been, like, older. They would have been, like, "oh, get her out — she wants to play with our things". I would have felt that from a very young age, kind of pushed away. I was pushed with me brothers, to the two little boys. And obviously, like, I wasn't a little boy.

We moved around a lot when I was younger. We moved from Clondalkin to an area near Tallaght. Then we moved back again. We were like Travellers. My father has a responsible job. He wasn't a very affectionate man. He felt it, I realise that now, but he didn't show it. His mother was the same. They weren't kind of a very huggy-kissy family.

I felt I was very sensitive. I do feel I was special. I think my mother knew that. There was just something extra, soft, about me. I wanted the affection all the time. And I wanted the approval of everybody in the house. Not just me mother. I wanted to be able to deal with me sisters, too. I remember the nightmares I used to have as a kid. I used to have dreams of the devil. At one stage I had a bed in me mother and father's room, because I was so insecure. But from a young age, I slept with my sister Denise, the second eldest. And even to this day, I'd have a very special bond with her. She'd be about six years older than me. And as I say I would have slept with her. Then, when we were separated, I was in a bed on me own, and it was really strange for me. I felt so weird. That is the only way I can describe it. I felt like a really weird child.

My first day in primary school, I'll never forget it. I was only four. But I can remember going in, and the first day I was roaring crying, screaming because my father was leaving me off and I didn't want to go in. The nun actually slapped me on the hands, because I was hysterical. And they had to call me sister, who would have been in sixth class. And she was, like, oh, will you fucking stop crying. I was just hysterical. I ended up forming a very special bond with that nun. I became very close with her.

All through primary school, I was in all the school plays. I just wanted to be somebody else. Somebody else completely. I always got the leads, because I can sing. I think that did help me express meself, but now I know I just wanted to be somebody else. A lot of addicts that I know are great actors. They love drama, poetry, things like that.

Primary school was strict because it was run by nuns. I wasn't very clever. I could never concentrate because I spent most of me time daydreaming. About different things. That would have held me back a lot at school, getting hassled by teachers for not doing homework and stuff. I know I started getting extremely fucked up in meself around the age of nine.

My mother can be controlling. But they weren't really that strict. I think one of the problems with me is that I got a lot of freedom, especially in me teenage years. I had an awful lot of freedom. I think it was because there was so many of us. We weren't really short of money. I didn't have a deprived childhood. She used to say to me, if you go up to bed at a certain time, we'll buy you this and we'll buy you that — but I was hyper, hyper.

I used to fight people an awful lot. People used to be saying I was a fucking terror, you know. I loved being rough. I don't know why it was because I'm not that type of person at all. I think I was so afraid of the way I was feeling about myself.

I would have felt that I wasn't being noticed in the house. I would always clean the house for me parents. Always. But it wasn't really because I wanted to do it. I wanted them to come and say, well done, good girl for doing that. I used to do that all the time. They used to come and say, Oh, Michelle's done this again.... it wasn't enough. I think I just wanted to be held and minded and somebody to tell me that everything was going to be OK. It's really weird. Then the different friends I would have. I had a special friend who lived on my road, Anne-Marie was her name, and I would have known her from a young age, up to secondary school.

From the age of nine, we used to play the normal games on the road, like rounders. But the girls were a lot older than I was. They would have been starting smoking, and I would be smoking with them. I loved that. I wanted to be like them, to be older. Me mother smokes, no one else in the house does. They're not really drinkers either. My mother is from the country. She's been living in Dublin a few years, but she has this thing about herself — she wants to be somebody she's not. She's very unsettled.

With the cigarettes, I would have started taking something to drink from a young age. I loved doing things that I know I wasn't supposed to do. I'd get into arguments when I was a kid. Even though I was getting given out to, I loved that. I loved the attention I was getting, because I was doing something wrong.

I loved the attention for being bold. When my mother would be giving out to me, secretly I'd be saying, well this is the way to get this woman's attention, you know.

It was the 80s, and you know yourself how it was — my elder sisters would be going out and meeting different people. They were all living their own lives. I was always stuck with the two younger lads.

I would have been a very outgoing kind of kid. I loved entertainment. I loved having a laugh. I was always real nice to everyone, and everyone was always going, what a lovely little girl. But inside I was thinking, no I'm not, I'm horrible. I felt, I couldn't stand me own skin, from a very young age. I just felt really strange about boys and men in general. I think it's because I wanted so much to be one of the girls. I was so pushed towards my two brothers because we were closer in age. And I couldn't understand why the two elder girls wouldn't let me hang out with them.

I went to secondary school in 1990. I was twelve just going on thirteen. I would have been drinking and all with the girls on me road. They would have been at the age, getting towards fifteen. They would be drinking like the ends of their Ma and Da's cans in the house. I remember feeling woozy, and loving it. My mother wouldn't have been very hard on me, because I was always so good in the house, cleaning up and all. The good girl outside and the bad girl inside.

I would have made friends in secondary school. First thing I went to secondary school, the girl who lived up the road from me, Anne-Marie, she would have been in the class. I felt at home then. I can remember me first day walking into the secondary school, and I remember seeing Anne-Marie's face, and thinking, it's OK now because she's in the class. I had another friend, Suzanne. This girl had epilepsy. I minded her the whole way through. I used to carry spoons around in me back pocket. I was always attracted to people who had problems. I'd carry a spoon around in case she had a fit. I'd be crying me eyes out because she had a fit. I'd be minding her, and I always had to be there.

I then began to feel I had a little network going, that I didn't need me mother's approval. The older girls I'd be hanging around with, they'd go in to tell my mother that they were after being at the Red Cow, drinking. And I loved all this, and I thought, God, she's great. They all would have went to her, and she's a very understanding person that way: she used to laugh with them.

After school, most days, all my friends would come around to my house, because my mother would let us smoke. She'd let us have our tea and toast, after school ... she was very understanding. And I would have had a lot of freedom. I was allowed stay out till late. I remember when I was sixteen, being able to stay out till half eleven. I was given a lot of freedom. They didn't think I would take the road that I did. There was a lot of trust.

I can remember at school, smoking. Just cigarettes. Drinking, things like that. Staying in me friend Suzanne's. Staying in her house, we'd go out drinking. Then me friends would have changed. I would have started hanging out with Amanda, she's still me friend today. Then there'd be Sharon, Stephanie, Linda. There was about eight of us. We were all the same year. From about thirteen, we'd be drinking. From about fourteen, it'd be hash.

It was this new thing, it would be, let's smoke this, you know. There wasn't anything about like, this is a drug that could ruin you. We knew nothing about it. We got drugs education at school, in Sixth Year, when it was far too late. It was like, ah, we'll just be mad, smoking hash, drinking and smoking cigarettes. I remember the disco, we'd got to — we'd fall into this disco puking our guts out. This was all brilliant. It was just a different life. I was an individual. I had all me friends around me. But I didn't need them, because I was finding all these new things out about meself.

I can't even remember what age I was when I took LSD. I was still at school ... it was kind of like, the drug thing was getting bigger. It was getting more known to all of us anyway. And we would all go to this disco and take LSD , and be out of our heads. We'd be drinking as well. It wasn't even that anyone would give it to us. We'd go looking for it. We'd heard about all these things. We would have known where to get it. I can't even remember how much it was. It wasn't dear. We'd get our pocket money and we'd buy it with that.

Then, when I was sixteen, my friend Anne-Marie was killed. Yeah, she was killed. She was knocked down. On Newland's Cross, just beside Bewley's Hotel in Tallaght. She was crossing the road. She was actually going down to get a packet of cigarettes. She was after being out sick all that week. We were all going in town on the Saturday. I rang her on the Friday evening about an hour before she was killed. She was saying, come on we'll go into town. She walked down to the shop to get the smokes, and she got killed. She was the only girl in her family. I could not understand why that happened to her. It was horrible, the funeral. It was really hard. It wasn't the same after that. She was dead. The way she was killed was horrific. The driver wasn't prosecuted. After that we tried to get a walkover bridge.

That would have been a very emotional time for all of us. But I think I was thriving on it as well. All the grief, the getting so involved, making sure everyone was OK. After that, I would have clung on to the likes of Amanda and Sharon and that. A year would have went by. And in that year, we started taking Ecstasy. Once I started taking Ecstasy, I didn't put drugs down.

We would have smoked hash all the time. In the toilets at school. We would have taken the Ecstasy and the LSD nearly every day. We'd be out of our heads. And my ma never noticed. After Ecstasy, it was, oh my God this is amazing. I loved it more than the LSD ... all my friends, we were all together, and it was just this feeling that all the hassles all around you were just gone. All the way I felt about meself was gone. With the LSD you'd be laughing a lot, the same with the hash. With the Ecstasy, it would have been the feelings that it gave you.

We would have taken it every weekend. My friends were going into the rave scene, in town, that would have been the big thing at that time. We used to come into school, with heads on us. We'd be brain-dead, completely. But we just plodded along. Me mother was getting called up to the school all the time. They knew I

such a thing, said Dr Spock. It makes the father out to be such a dragon. Yet it reflected the notion that father was the lawmaker, and the ultimate deterrent.

Many plays and dramas of the mid-century — typified by J.B. Priestley in England and John B. Keane in Ireland — emphasised the stern, sometimes tyrannical order of family life. This would be characterised by a conflict over a family meal, in which Father and Mother would preside over the proceedings, and some terrible drama would erupt in the course of this act of bourgeois respectability (the daughter would announce a pregnancy, although the word "pregnant" was not used publicly until about 1960, or the son would declare he was going to Philadelphia in the morning).

Parents in fiction (though seldom in autobiography) were indeed sometimes seen as tyrannical. John B. Keane, the popular Irish playwright who has captured the essence of Irish rural society, wrote an extraordinarily powerful play in the early 1960s called "Big Maggie". Big Maggie was the absolute monarch of all she surveyed: a dominatrix of a widow woman who ruled her grown-up children with a rod of iron, doling them out small sums of money whenever she cared to, controlling and directing them as she desired. The drama involves their ultimate, tardy rebellion against this despot, and John B. wrote a later coda to the play in which Big Maggie explains that she was the way she was simply because she was embittered by repressive experiences — inevitably by the Catholic Church — that she had undergone.

A whole generation of younger parents determined that they would not be "Big Maggies", whether they had seen the play or not. They would not be tyrants to their children, but friends. They would be gentler and nicer to their kids. They would not be controlling and repressive, but imaginative and encouraging. This, in any case, was what the school of Benjamin Spock advised. At one level, parenting did begin to improve in the post-Spock period. Spock spawned a new generation of babycare books in his image. Parents did become more enlightened, and the whole concept of mindless authoritarianism — "do it because I say so" — began to disappear.

But in the course of this change, parents lost caste and position. They began to feel that they had less and less control, or even influence, over their children. The outside culture diminished the influence of parents and inflated the influence of television, the fashion industry, the music industry, the media, and the sex-drugs-rock-'n-roll industry. The State has increasingly encroached on family policy, sometimes for the better — in child health, for example — but nevertheless, ever diminishing the parental role. Feminism challenged the hegemony of fathers — patriarchy became a very bad word indeed — who were, in any case, ever more marginalised by the expansion of the one-parent family. Educational psychologists now say that the peer group plays just as significant a role in the formation of young people as parents. It is small wonder that the most usual feeling that parents have, when faced with a drug problem in the family, is sheer helplessness.

Dr John O'Connor, the Director of Clinical Practice at the National Drug Treatment Centre in Dublin says that he gets the impression that parents have been so intimidated by the social changes that have occurred that they are terrified of asserting their authority at all. "I think that sometimes parents are now afraid to parent. As a parent, you have to *be* a parent. You cannot be an older brother or sister. You have to have boundaries. I think people are basically good, and they want to do their best. But often, people have to be shown a way."

Maura Russell of the Rutland Clinic in Dublin echoes that. "Young people today, their parents came through a particular age and time, a time of more liberal attitudes to parenting, so to apply stricter boundaries to their kids is hard for them. Their style of parenting is to be buddies with their kids. I am not suggesting that the stricter way was, overall, better: it was just different. We have to recognise that."

Yet she feels, in talking to parents, that often "they don't know how to deal with their kids any more. That's across the board. People just don't know how to deal with that very difficult period of adolescence, and take their kids through it.

"They don't know how to manage the problems that emerge in adolescence. They don't know how to make the distinctions between exploring and experimenting with drugs and drink, which is part of the curiosity of adolescence. They don't know how far to go as between trusting and knowing when to intervene." Parenting is a reflection of the wider society, anyhow, she points out. There is no institution now — political, religious, familial — which "grounds" people, which "evokes a sense of respect, or even fear."

"So it is much more difficult for parents. Because they don't have anything to hold their structures. Before it was easier, even for a single parent: you didn't have to be an old-fashioned stick-in-the-mud to set these structures, because everybody was doing it the same way. It was the more unusual circumstance to find somebody with a very flexible approach to parenting." Old-fashioned parenting, for example, meant a set time for meals, every single evening, with the family gathered around the table, the children with their hands washed, and being given instruction on table manners. Significantly, the makers of the Oxo beef cube — a culinary accessory to meat dishes which has been on the go since the Crimean War (Florence Nightingale recommended it) — made the decision to withdraw their "family meal" television commercial in August 1999.

Variations on the Oxo family meal commercial had been transmitted for forty-three years, but the marketing men announced that most people no longer identify with the concept of a family meal. It is out of date. Most families eat their evening meal separately, some on a tray in front of the TV, some in their bedrooms playing computer games, some using takeaways, or heating frozen snacks in the microwave.

The regular family meal was certainly a symbol of family discipline and family authority. A study undertaken at Oxford Polytechnic during the 1980s showed that this is precisely what adolescents disliked about the family meal — that it called them to account, and was likely to be an occasion of conflict, usually about clothes or hair lengths.

We have to deal with life as it is now, and the Oxo family meal tradition is indeed gone, and will probably not reappear. Yet it was the kind of occasion which helped — or, as we would now say, "empowered" — parents to exercise some authority and control of adolescents, and also, to observe generally how things are going. "Kids can get away with a great amount of drugs without anybody noticing," Maura Russell says. In this she includes the abuse of alcohol, which she feels parents are too laid back about. Parents certainly are worried about opiate drugs, but "alcohol is just not seen as dangerous, by parents. Their kids can drink, and they're not that worried. They're pretty cool about it. But parents should be worrying about alcohol intake at thirteen, fourteen and fifteen. I think they need education about the whole nature of drugs. The conversations need to start about twelve or thirteen. Are drugs being offered to you at school? What do you think about it? That kind of conversation really does need to go on."

I failed to do any of this myself, as a parent. I passively left all discussions about drugs to the school, which was a well-ordered Catholic school in West London. The school took a pro-active line on drug prevention, but in retrospect I realise that Maura Russell is right. That kind of conversation does need to go on at home, too.

Grainne Kenny — who is no relation, by the way — has been involved in drug education since the late 1970s. She runs an educational forum, Eurad (for Europe Against Drugs) in Dun Laoghaire, Co Dublin which has regular links in other European countries, particularly Sweden and Switzerland. (It is not associated with the European Community.) Grainne is a widow with three grown-up children, and she has twenty years experience of talking to young people about drugs.

Hardly anyone has ever started a dangerous drug habit with heroin, Grainne points out. Young children are horrified by the idea of someone sticking a needle in their arm for pleasure, so you don't start by warnings, or conversations, about drugs like heroin. You start by discussing the "gateway drugs", which she categorises as alcohol, cigarettes and cannabis. Virtually everyone who finishes up with a serious drug habit has started with these three (not absolutely everybody: Lauren Rodgers, the sixteen-year-old girl from Derby who died of a fatal dose of heroin, never smoked cigarettes). But over ninety per cent of heroin users also smoke cigarettes.

I am politically neutral on the subject of cannabis. As I have indicated in earlier chapters, I find that hash smokers are bores — the French word, *stupefiant*, rather aptly describes the condition rendered by dope. As does the American word for a blockhead — a dope.

But there are some active campaigners in Britain, and some in Ireland, too, who argue for the legalisation, or decriminalisation of cannabis, on the grounds that it would be safer to remove from prohibition a "soft" drug that is widely used. And that it is wrong to criminalise citizens for indulging in a pastime that is arguably no worse than a weekend session in the pub.

Many perfectly respectable (and middle-aged) people do smoke cannabis as a weekend relaxant, and I have a colleague whose wife, when dying of ovarian cancer, found relief from pain in a joint of marijuana. So I do not know what the political answer to the cannabis question is, and I would support the suggestion, made in Britain, that there should be an independent Royal Commission to investigate the subject.

Moreover, since dealers in cannabis often supply heroin, and other harder drugs as well, it would be sensible to separate the "soft" from the "hard". My younger son has told me that while the penalties for possessing cannabis are so similar to those for possessing heroin (three years in jail as opposed to five years in jail), there is no "incentive" not to move from cannabis to heroin, in dealing or using.

But Grainne Kenny does not accept the thesis that we should be more liberal about so-called "soft" drugs: soft drugs pave the way for hard drugs, she emphasises. Soft drugs get young people into the sub-culture of drugs. Besides, she says, these drugs are not so "soft" after all. "Dutch skunk", a currently fashionable species of cannabis is, says, Grainne "stronger than a hit of heroin". And before we look at the impact of heroin, we must, in her view, honestly examine the workings of its main gateway drug, cannabis. And the main gateway drug to cannabis is cigarettes. "If you smoke cigarettes, there's at least a fifty per cent chance that you will go on to cannabis." Cigarette smoking "teaches" young people the art of inhaling: the youngsters who say "I tried a bit of blow and it didn't do anything for me" are those who are not yet seasoned cigarette smokers, who have not yet learned how to inhale. You have to draw cannabis down into your lungs — "the longer you hold it, the more value you get, because it goes up to the brain, because it's fat soluble, and the more you can get into the brain, the better the high." (The brain is a fatty tissue and responds to a fat-soluble drug.)

Cannabis, Grainne Kenny maintains, could actually be worse for your health than heroin. A person urinates heroin out of their system in a matter of hours, she explains. Cannabis, being fat-soluble, rather than water-soluble, takes between four and six weeks to leave the body. "The very first joint of cannabis that a youngster smokes — 50 per cent of it would leave the brain within seven days. You won't be high, but your brain will retain it, and you'll be slightly stoned. Your concentration will not be great. But it takes between four and six weeks for the other fifty per cent to leave your body." So when people smoke hash frequently, they have a slow build-up, and they are never quite drug-free. When they stop using cannabis, it will take from between eight to ten months for the drug fully to leave their system.

A joint of cannabis is ten to twenty times stronger than the cigarette in which it is smoked. "The carcinogens in the tobacco prepare the lungs for the carcinogens in cannabis." A joint of cannabis contains 2,000 chemicals and can lead to cancer of the tongue, mouth, throat and lungs, to chromosome damage and to the early onset of senility.

Grainne showed me slides of the brains of cannabis smokers — their vessels and synaptic clefts darkened and broken, in contrast to the clear brains of non-smokers. "These guys were smoking very mild stuff," she said, of the subjects whose brains had been affected. "These joints were about two per cent, which is what the Beatles were smoking in the 1960s. You won't buy these today — they are specially grown for research. The minimum on the market today would be about 15 per cent." The Dutch skunk currently so favoured will produce a joint which is 40 per cent narcotic, and gives a stronger hit than heroin.

Liberals who advance the cause of cannabis legalisation will perhaps dispute some of these claims, or consider them over-stated; or perhaps compare the impact of cannabis to the impact of perfectly legal alcohol, which certainly does a great deal of damage in terms of crime, accidental deaths, violence and cruelty to children, let alone to the alcoholic himself. I am open to hearing both sides of the argument, but if we are to be made drug-aware, as parents, family members, or just well-informed individuals, then it is surely right that tutorials on cannabis, which certainly does act as a gateway drug to heroin (and other opiates) are extremely helpful.

Anecdotally, I have also observed that those recovering heroin addicts who continue to use cannabis do not recover. If dope is a gateway drug, it is also a re-admission ticket back down the darkening road of heroin abuse. At the same time, while most heroin users have started on cannabis, not all cannabis users go on to use heroin.

Yet it is when young people are introduced to the sub-culture of drugs that they become susceptible to trying the whole menu. Availability and susceptibility are the two factors which make an addict, Grainne Kenny affirms. The availability is there: ecstasy, LSD, speed, cocaine, crack cocaine and heroin are all down the road from cannabis, although some may take ecstasy without trying cannabis first. Addicts have spoken frequently about their experimentations with such an array of drugs around the age of twelve, thirteen, fourteen.

It is very difficult for a parent to prevent something which is all around, and in the culture. The notion that drug abuse only affects either decadent aristocrats — the likes of the Marquess of Bristol, who died in his forties after spending £10 million on heroin and cocaine — or really deprived and depressed housing estates is now somewhat out of date. Hard drugs are everywhere now. In England, heroin flourishes most vividly in genteel market towns like Cheltenham and Bath. Quiet little Norfolk is awash with serious drug abuse. Parents do not have the power to control the culture outside the home, and quite often feel unable to control their adolescent young inside it.

Yet they can be watchful about signs of trouble, or special moments of vulnerability. That period of changing schools, from primary school, to secondary, can be a vulnerable time. Children go from the cosiness and comfort of a little school, where there is no real stress, to the strains of a big school, where they suddenly feel insignificant and are under a lot more pressure. If they are bullied at school, or in the playground, this can make them vulnerable. If they are anxious and uncertain, and want to impress "the big boys" (or the big girls), they may be vulnerable to doing the big kids' bidding.

The most dangerous drug pusher is not a tout at the school gates in a dirty raincoat: it is another school pupil in the "honeymoon phase" of drug use. "It may be somebody very nice, the leader of the pack, a lovely-looking girl or a fine fellow, and everybody is round that person, smoking a bit of dope, not getting into any trouble, their grades are all right," Grainne Kenny observes. "No problem. And they're the people, then, who are the main suppliers of drugs at schools. It is somebody at the honeymoon phase who has started to use more and more heavily, and has the stuff for distribution. And the kids think, well, I'd never be a drug addict, I'd never inject heroin — but where's the harm in a bit of hash?"

It is obvious that parents need to talk to teachers about what is going on at school, since no school now is free of drugs. That they need to know what signs to watch for: the drop in school grades, truancy, the loss of interest in work or hobbies, the lack of concentration, the tiredness, the radical changes in behaviour, the new friends — sometimes older — the mood swings, the cravings for sweet things (a side-effect of opiates), the unusual smells, the rashes around the mouth and the runny noses, the continuous coughs and chest infections and the obsessive secrecy.

Yet many of these are part of the normal phases of adolescence: I was a truant from school, I lost interest in work, I went in for secret societies, I was unspeakably awful to my widowed mother and was in every way completely peculiar at about the age of fifteen, and I certainly wasn't on drugs at the time (I hadn't even discovered smoking and drinking yet). So it is may be very difficult to know for sure, and it is all too easy to go into denial. The normal response of a normal parent, on being told that their child is using drugs is outrage, and the loyal defence that "my son — daughter — would never do that".

Grainne recommends that parents use methods of surveillance on adolescents: examining schoolbags and searching their rooms. For some parents this seems too untrusting (and some of us who remember the stern surveillance techniques used in former times — diaries read, lockers ransacked, at boarding school — quite repellent). But it is another option. "It is not fair to trust your children too much, " she says.

Adolescents need time and supervision. They should not have too much pocket money — working mothers are inclined to guiltily over-compensate with money in lieu of time. Schoolchildren should not, if possible, have to come home to an empty house. This may be difficult for parents to arrange, but lack of supervision is a definite factor in early drug experimentation. Schools once routinely offered "after-school study" to pupils, where they could do their homework at the school until six p.m. It is worth reviving.

If there is a bereavement in the family, the adolescent will be more vulnerable. They will also be more vulnerable if there is a divorce or separation. Grainne Kenny, who is also a qualified bereavement counsellor, insists that children must be involved in the whole process of a family death, as with a parental separation or divorce.

It doesn't always do to minimise the impact of a divorce too much either. "I remember my mother saying that Dad and she were separating, and it was all going to be OK, it was quite amicable," says one recovering addict. "But it wasn't OK, and it wasn't amicable." The mother was trying to put a good face on it, and shielding the children, but the son then blamed himself when conflict continued to erupt between the separated parents. Until he found the comfort of heroin, that is, always the great comforter.

If there is someone else in the family with an addiction problem, it is important to understand that this will make the children more susceptible. Studies done indicate that individuals with a drug habit come from families where there has been addiction. This may be a very wide canvas: in Ireland, as in Scotland (as in Scandinavia) there are few families which have not included a serious alcoholic. But addiction to tranquillisers or any other mood-altering drug must also now be considered. In the 1980s, doctors over-prescribed tranquillisers quite irresponsibly, particularly to mothers, it seems. (There was a dreadful pharmaceutical advert in a medical magazine showing a stressed-out young mother in a ghastly housing estate. The caption read: "You can't change her environment. But you can change her mood.") If the mothers or the grandmothers are on tranquillisers, it is more likely that the youngsters will use an opiate drug.

It is sensible to warn children if there is a problem in the family. ("Look, Kiddo, you know your aunt/dad/granny drank the Liffey dry in their time — so do watch out for that family weakness gene.") Grainne

Kenny says that it should be explained properly to children if anyone in the family is on medication: medication is for sick people, but it is not for well people. Moreover, all medication has some unwelcome side-effects. Grainne believes the bathroom medicine cabinet should be locked, if there are any drugs that could be abused. She even thinks that mothers should watch their handbags, if these contain medication that could be abused. This may sound paranoid, but users do remember having their first high from nicking a parental benzo.

When parents come to realise, and admit, that there is a serious drug problem, they feel, according to a study done for the Institute for the Study of Drug Dependence in London, angry, guilty, pained: they feel a sense of loss and betrayal. "I feel guilty because I feel it's all my fault." "Anger, angry that you can't do anything. My first response was anger that he was so weak." One father said: "I simply can't talk about it."

Mothers and fathers may react differently, as will different siblings. "The fathers on the whole just did not want to know because they could not cope with the idea," one mother is quoted in the ISDD study. It is a common experience, when attending a group meeting for parents of drug abusers, that it is predominantly composed of mothers (and sisters) who attend. At one London meeting, a father noted "about thirty women and about four men". This is replicated in Dublin, where "the mammies and the sisters" predominate at family support groups. Interestingly, this was also true of temperance meetings or prayer groups for alcoholics in

189

the early years of the twentieth century: dominated by women, praying for the menfolk.

Parents may differ about the response and treatment for an addict; addicts are manipulative — as all recovering addicts will themselves admit — and can deliberately divide parents. It is more common for the mother to "side with the kids", against the father, and that will be exploited. It will, says Grainne Kenny, be the mother who is the more likely "enabler", slipping the addict money, behind the father's back. But if the parents are in any way divided, it weakens the strategy in helping the addict to stop.

If the parent is a single parent, Maura Russell at the Rutland thinks it's a good idea to involve another senior family member — an aunt, uncle, or an elder sibling. "Rarely if ever do the intervention by yourself," she advises parents. "Always try and have another member of the family alongside. For the parent to child relationship, the problem of drugs should not be tackled one-to-one."

Confrontational techniques do not work, parents are advised. Pleas and cajoling may also fall on deaf ears. Recovering addicts themselves often conclude that at the end of the day it is only when the pain of drug abuse outweighs the pleasures that people are willing to contemplate quitting. The family strategy has to be finding ways of helping the addict as a person, of supporting him in treatment, of reassuring them that they are loved and cared for, while not facilitating or enabling. I have encountered parents who have called in a private drugs counsellor to arbitrate, as it were, in the situation, and it has helped. The parent, or parents, also need to affirm their rights to their own space. They are entitled to live in their own home without having to put everything under lock and key, because heroin addicts steal, however sweet and honest they may be by nature.

Love and care lavished on the addict can, paradoxically, have a negative effect on siblings in the family. The other children may feel overlooked and aggrieved. "I feel there can be a great deal of resentment that can start in the family because the addicted person is getting all the attention for a long time. Everything is revolving around that person or that person's sickness or addiction, and the others think, well, we're behaving perfectly all right, and they don't take the slightest notice. I don't come into it, do I?" Some siblings will reject the addict: Thomas, a Dubliner with HIV told me, resentfully — "My brother lives in Limerick. I've never seen the inside of his home." Other siblings will become protectors, and enter into a kind of collusion with the addict, covering up for him (or her).

There is standard advice given about not maintaining secrecy. Recovering addicts themselves say that they were helped when their habit was out in the open (and sometimes they really do want to be found out). Counsellors say it causes more trouble when the secret is concealed from some members of the family: it causes divisions and alliances which the addict exploits. Families are even urged to talk about the heroin habit quite openly in society at large: but many families find this an anguishing order. "I just can't tell the neighbours — can't, can't, can't," a mother at a Dublin parents' group said to me. "I can't bear for them to know." I find this altogether understandable: families are entitled to their privacy, and heroin addicts are, after all, stigmatised. But if a habit ends up with a death, and a recorded verdict in the Coroner's Court, the element of privacy will be well gone. People really do have to judge for themselves.

Some parents have reported their son or daughter to the police — heroin is an illegal drug, and most users are also involved in dealing, and in criminal activities — but the majority of parents shrink from it. I would find it very difficult to go that far in "tough love". Some parents come to feel that the addiction problem in a child is really a 'family problem', and seek therapy for the whole family. One couple I met recommended this: "It just helped all of us to start expressing our feelings and healing problems of the past."

Quite often parents do not know about the habit, or do not know until it is late in the day, and the young person is in his twenties and living away from home anyway. Soft drugs may begin in the early teens, but the heroin habit can start at university. There are times when families cannot influence or control the situation any more, and it is down to the individual to work through his addiction. This is hard, but sometimes the advice is — "let go". The support groups for parents and family members can be very helpful indeed. The parents who attend these meetings are usually very concerned people and they learn a lot from sharing their sorrows.

This problem is not going to go away. The generations born before the 1960s did not know what drug problems were, because there was hardly any mass availability. They grew up in a world of automatic parental (and wider family) authority, backed by social authority, which could be either good or bad according to who was wielding it, but was probably quite effective in supervision and protection. The children of today are growing up to face a very different world to that of their parents' generation, so there is a greater need than ever before for parents to be more educated, more aware and more pro-active about the grief and destruction that drugs can bring.

A key word in the prevention of early teenage drug abuse.

Supervision, supervision, supervision, supervision, supervision, supervision, supervision, supervision, supervision, supervision, supervision, supervision, supervision, supervision, supervision, supervision, supervision.

Who are they with? What are they doing? What time are they coming home? Is there a responsible adult checking on them regularly?

Supervision, supervision, supervision, supervision, supervision.

Supervision.

(The formula also works in preventing teenage pregnancy.)

Chapter Ten

Some Answers, Some Questions, Some Proposals for Change

When the prestige of state and religion is low, men are free, but they find freedom intolerable and seek new ways to enslave themselves, through drugs or depression.
— Camilla Paglia. Sex and Destiny.

If taking heroin is an irrational act, why assume that rationality and logic will cure it?
— Arnold S. Trebach. The Heroin Solution.

I embarked on a quest to find an answer to this question: why does a nice, intelligent, lively, and cherished young person choose to stick a hypodermic needle in his arm in an action which leads to his death? There is always a mysterious element in human behaviour, but I have learned much on this melancholy quest. Some of the answers I found were personal, some social and political. Questioning the use of heroin also led me to much self-examination. I think many of us try to escape from life, in one way or another. Why do we have such a compulsive need to "get out of ourselves"? Some of us have used alcohol rather than opiates to escape from ourselves, a less immediately fatal yet behaviourally more vicious drug. Alcoholics hurt others. Heroin addicts hurt themselves.

Sometimes this need to escape is put down to poor social conditions. Yet if we compare the 1950s with the 1980s and 1990s, as Oliver James has done in his book examining the increase in depression which has accompanied the rise in living standards, we find that when social conditions were worse, people seemed better able to face the difficulties of life.

"Availability and susceptibility" are the two logical reasons for heroin use, as described by Grainne Kenny, who has been working on the drug question for over twenty years. The more a drug is available, the more people will try it. If an individual is susceptible to dependency or addiction, he is likely to become an addict. (It is appropriate to use the pronoun "he" since there are three times as many heroin deaths among males as among females.) Once an addict, dangerous choices will be made because the desire for the drug is greater than any other consideration. But again, the gender agenda is relevant: males are generally more inclined to make riskier choices. Even among children under ten, fatal accidents among boys is three times that of girls, largely because of this male risk factor.

I cannot impose upon my nephews' lives my judgements of their motives; and in any case it is not for me to judge. But I believe that their deaths represented availability and susceptibility respectively. Conor's death was due to the availability of heroin and Patrick's to his susceptibility to addiction.

To Conor, a brave but reckless personality, an inventive practical joker with a try-anything-once approach to life, heroin was interesting, it was pleasurable, and it was available. In his situation, I would have done exactly as he did.

A friend of his told me a story about how he and Conor experimented with the smoking of heroin. The friend bumped into Conor of an evening and they decided to smoke some dope in Conor's downtown office. Conor went off to buy the cannabis, a "soft drug" which many thirty-somethings regard as the equivalent of having a pint. When he returned he said to his friend: "the supplier was fresh out of cannabis. But he sold me some skag (heroin) instead." So the pair of them smoked the heroin. Conor's friend was violently ill as a consequence and never tried it again. Unfortunately, perhaps, Conor had no reaction of nausea.

To smoke cannabis is an accepted, normalised part of life among young professionals today; my younger media colleagues regard it as reassuringly harmless. It is considered absurd and authoritarian that it should still be criminalised, and dangerous that the same dealer who sells street cannabis may also deal in heroin. Perhaps this is so. But it is also true that many users of hard drugs became "opiate aware" through the use of cannabis. It was hash which opened the opiate receptors of the mind, and got them into the habit of turning on, and getting stoned. And once you like the idea of getting stoned, then, as Tam Stewart writes in her autobiographical book about heroin use, "you are never stoned enough, and when you are you are unconscious".

Availability: if heroin had been available, I would have used it, when younger and single. I came very close to trying it in mature middle age. The occultist writer Aleister Crowley's description of heroin as bringing — "this sensation of infinite power ... The feeling of mastery increases to such a point that nothing matters at all", is regarded as almost classically exact: this is a very seductive drug. But more than mastery of the universe, the removal of anxiety is a huge allure. Many respectable middle-aged people would take heroin, for that reason, if it were easily available to them. When knocked senseless by grief, one of the bereaved mothers of a heroin user said to me — "God knows, I wish I could take some myself, to get out of my tormented head."

Conor was not using heroin long enough to be an addict; he was still a recreational user. But even recreational users of heroin go into denial. Marie-Louise, Conor's sister, tackled him on several occasions about heroin, but he denied it categorically. "Get a grip," he told her. "I have too much going for me to do that kind of shit." There is a division between the conscious and the unconscious mind when it comes to drug use (alcohol, too). The logical mind knows that a drug is dangerous and will deny its use. But the other part of the mind, which runs on feelings and impulses, will go on doing it.

A year before his death, Marie-Louise heard that Conor was experimenting with smoking heroin; she "went ballistic" and reported him to the drug squad. This can be a very helpful intervention. A man who feels he has a lot going for himself will indeed sober up when cautioned by the police. The guards could not find sufficient evidence, and therefore were unable to issue the caution. It is my belief that the police, in Ireland and in Britain, are not particularly exercised by individual heroin use. They go after the big fish, and the "drug barons" like Edward Scanlon, an apparently respectable Cork family man who got twenty-two years in jail, in 1999, for importing huge hauls of a range of drugs into Ireland. But, according to the anecdotal evidence of heroin users, the police tend to leave individual users alone. Heroin users say that getting busted is less of a risk than it used to be.

Yet the problem, essentially, with heroin use is that it is demand-driven, not supply-driven. Big drug gangsters made heroin available in the first place, in the 1980s. But most people who use it today seem to go looking for it. Edward Scanlon could quite reasonably argue that he was merely meeting a demand for a commodity. Putting him behind bars will only have the effect of temporarily increasing the street price, which will, paradoxically, increase the amount of crime.

Huge amounts of heroin have been seized, internationally, since the modern phase of the "war on drugs" began, in the 1970s. One American source cites the sum of ten billion dollars a year in law enforcement fighting drugs. These heroin confiscations do nothing to stop the habit, and overall, the street price has continued to fall (a hit which costs £10 today cost £50 or £60 in the early 1980s), which implies that availability continues unabated. You can only reduce or modify drug use by deterring the demand, rather than stemming the supply. The most effective way of halting heroin use is by discouraging demand, which may have to be done — as the great temperance movements of the nineteenth century were done — through some kind of moral crusade. At a personal, individual level, the police arrest or caution of an individual user may cause him to revise, or eventually stop, his habit, and therefore may, almost paradoxically, be more effective than seeking to stem the supply.

Conor was just not to know that a hit of heroin would kill him. He was a risk-taking person, but not a self-destructive one. His friends all said that it was simply very, very unlucky; even "a freak accident". But I write these words for one overwhelming purpose: that anyone who chooses to take a hit of heroin must be informed that it can kill. It is not mere alarmism to point that out. It happens. And the misery that follows that death is, for many years, quite literally unspeakable.

There is recovery from a heroin habit; but for those bereaved, there may be no recovery from a heroin death. If Conor had known the consequences, he would have drawn back from using, and stopped: I am certain of that. That is what turned Tam Stewart around, as she tells it in her autobiography. There was just a dawning realisation that "no short-term thrill is worth the loss of your life", when your life is before you.

For darling, high-spirited Conor, it was all about availability. For his sweet-natured, lovely younger brother Patrick, I believe it was susceptibility.

Patrick was a gentle guy with a poet's temperament. I reproach myself for not taking a closer interest in Patrick; for when a young person loses a parent at a susceptible age — as I have had cause to mention, my brother died when PK was fifteen — another family member should try to compensate, supporting both the surviving parent and the bereaved child. Young people need mentors; they are launched too soon into a highly individualistic world in which they are expected to define themselves by their choices — this being the core of our contemporary existentialism. In former times, young people had tutors, guardians, employers to whom they were apprenticed, or, if they were religious, spiritual directors.

The heroin users who make a continuing good recovery are, very noticeably, those who find some kind of helping mentor, be it a counsellor or a sponsor within a twelve-step programme; or just a special friend who offers guidance and advice. I will not say that Patrick's friends let him down, but it is a generalised truth that when a heroin user begins to move more deeply into addiction, the non-using friends drift away, and other addicts become the mainstream friends. In his book on "Street Drugs", written from an objective and non-judgemental point of view, Andrew Tyler nonetheless advises that if you want to stop using heroin, you must stay away from other users.

Many recovering addicts have spoken to me about this "circle of friends" phenomenon, and I remember something similar, anyway, from my own drinking days. When you are drinking, you can't stand to be with sober folks. When you are using a drug, you gravitate towards those who are similar. Margaret, a recovering addict now firmly committed to Narcotics Anonymous, says that even at the age of thirteen or fouteen — "you always know your own". You know by a look, a glance, a gesture, a joke, who will be your peers and supporters in a habit.

One of PK's closest (non-drug-using) friends recalled that the heroin habit started for my younger nephew around 1991 or 1992. "Before that it was just hash." This friend of Patrick's also tried heroin, once, with him but didn't care for it. Why did he try it? "It was something you do. You can dabble to a certain extent, but once it begins to take a hold of you, then it gets difficult." This friend had a kind of vision of Patrick "drifting out to sea", his old friends sometimes trying to claw him back, and then the tide of heroin returning to claim him. But once heroin claimed a person, the friend said, you didn't say any more about it. It was the person's choice. "I knew

Patrick was doing it, and he probably knew that I knew, but we didn't talk about it." He would disappear suddenly, and say he'd be back; he might and he might not. You knew where he was. At the end, he was exhausted with the whole thing, getting it, scoring, coming down, getting it again, scoring .... This friend knew that his father's death had been deeply significant for PK.

"Patrick was a much deeper, nicer person than Conor and I put together," Marie-Louise says. For him, heroin was an escape. He took a year out from Trinity College — the first member of our family to attend that august institution — and went to New York. Heroin was amongst his peers; he tried it and became dependent. It helped his ultra-sensitive nature to cope with life.

Nobody is to blame, directly, for Patrick's death: it was an appalling tragedy which is a not unusual outcome of heroin addiction. But I feel critical about the kind of medical care he received. After Conor's death, Patrick sought medical help for his problem, and he was prescribed the replacement drug, methadone. Methadone seems to be regarded, sometimes, as a cure-all treatment for heroin addiction. It is nothing of the sort. It is often prescribed because it is the only treatment available. If methadone was advertised it would be marketed thus: "Got a heroin problem? Reach for new, improved Methadone! Say goodbye to injection worries or smack cravings now!"

But methadone — known among opiate users as "phy", the brand name being Physeptone — is another dangerous drug, and can be as dangerous as, sometimes more dangerous than, heroin. It should only be used in closely monitored circumstances. Patrick was given a prescription of methadone over a Christmas period when there could be no monitoring of his blood or urine. Strangely, he might not have died if he had stuck to heroin, although no one can say for sure. But he had been using heroin for many years. Unlike Conor, he was an experienced user.

Patrick Kenny's death was not a heroin death; it was a heroin/methadone polydrug death, as the pathologists' report indicates. This is a more common form of fatality — twice as many people die from the cocktail of methadone and heroin than from heroin alone.

Conor's death was an accident, but PK's overdose could have been have been prevented. Poor darling Patrick, devastated by his brother's death, tried, pathetically, to make an effort to quit heroin by starting this methadone programme on his own. At the end of my quest, I became convinced that Patrick would have needed to go into a rehab clinic or hospital to start a programme under professional supervision. He was in too much trouble with addiction to be given a bottle of takeaway methadone over the Christmas period. It was a great pity that during the holiday period when the facility for monitoring his urine was closed down, that some responsible person was not appointed to supervise the methadone intake. A doctor who appoints a "methadone monitor" to an addict going on to Methadone Maintenance should be certain that the methadone monitor is not another heroin addict. I am sure Patrick was treated in good faith, but there is an awful lot of room for more knowledge about the treatment of heroin addicts.

And I believe that we must debate the question of allowing doctors to treat heroin addicts, in certain cases, with medically prescribed heroin (diamorphine), as Ray Byrne also concludes in his study of methadone. "Harm reduction" is now an agreed aim of drug policy, and this is one possible way of reducing harm. Where a heroin addict is so deeply into the drug, so helplessly dependent that he cannot, yet, give it up, the most sensible form of harm reduction is to prescribe diamorphine, under such carefully controlled medical circumstances that it cannot leak into street use. It would certainly save lives.

This treatment is available, in restricted circumstances, in Britain. We should raise the question of whether legislation should be introduced to make it possible in Ireland.

In the melancholy matter of drug addiction, we are learning all the time. Sometimes the hard way; the hardest, bitterest way of all.

There just was so much we didn't know.

"In the early 1980s," says Fintan, who used heroin for eight years, "we had no negative role-models." The drug availability began in earnest in the early 1980s. "There weren't people hanging around, gaunt and waving syringes full of blood. It didn't seem to have negative consequences, though there were some drug awareness programmes in schools — you know, 'don't touch heroin'. But we touched heroin, and the sky didn't fall on your head. It felt immensely pleasurable. You thought, then, I can get away with this. They were lying to me. It's not going to cause problems. And it didn't — at the beginning."

Fintan remembers those times in the 80s, "when there was a huge and very open drug scene at the Belfield bar" — that is, around University College Dublin. "It was like the fall of the Roman Empire — with this demarcation:

on one side, there were the engineering students, who just drank pints. On the other side, every druggy in south Dublin, and a few from north Dublin, chopping out lines (of heroin and cocaine) on the tables.

"But today, everyone knows someone who has been completely screwed up by drugs. By now, everyone of my age (the thirties) has been to a drug-related, or suicide-related, funeral. Back then, it was just an alternative way of life." The "great Nirvana" among the student set, Fintan recalls, was represented by the speedball — the mixture of heroin and cocaine. Until John Belushi died, there were "no negative role-models" to highlight this down-side. (John Belushi, an American comedian and actor, died in 1982 aged thirty-three. He had taken a speedball. He became a kind of negative drug icon in the tradition of self-destructive showbiz personalities. The death of Janis Joplin, from a fatal, though accidental, dose of heroin might also have been a "negative role model", except Janis Joplin died in 1970, before drugs became sufficiently widespread that others could identify with her death.)

At least, by the end of the century, we can no longer plead ignorance. Just as we all ought to know that drinking and driving is a dangerous, often fatal combination which is not acceptable behaviour, so we all ought to know that illegal drugs carry particular risks, can be fatal, and are especially dangerous for those who might be vulnerable to addiction.

We all need drug education — I certainly did. I was so ignorant about the drug effect that I was gladdened to see Patrick take a glass of wine. "If he's drinking wine," I thought, "he can't be on drugs all the time." I thought, in the profoundness of my stupidity, that one form of intoxicant would disbar another. "Drink more wine," I would say to him, thinking I was encouraging the lesser of the two evils. It is only since I went on my drug education quest that I learned that polydrug abuse is the most common form of drug abuse. Users add alcohol to all the other cocktail of drugs. One does not disbar another.

I feel that a lot more thought needs to go into the way drug education is done. I would like to see less political posturing and more reflectiveness in the matter of drugs. The drug field falls into the "prohibitionist" and "libertarian" camp. But this is an area in which we may indeed have to find a third way, and keep looking at what works; and keep looking, too, beyond the superficial, even beyond the mere rational. Drug taking is not a rational decision; why should there always be a rational solution?

You can't just concentrate on the horror stories. Young schoolchildren learning about drugs should not just be given blanket dire warnings about dangers to health and life. This approach has not worked, with young people, with cigarettes. As far as I can see, virtually all young people smoke, and yet virtually all young people have been subjected to anti-cigarette propaganda. This has been ineffective for a variety of reasons, but one of them is that the approach to cigarette smoking has not been honest. The horrors, the penalties and the pain that can follow from smoking cigarettes are emphasised. The fact that smoking is pleasurable is ignored. Tobacco is comforting and supportive, and the act of smoking brims with camaraderie. It is a matchless accessory for the shy and the aesthete alike. It bristles with sex-appeal and the interplay of flirtation. The penalties of smoking are mostly too long-term (bronchitis at sixty? heart disease? cancer in old age? who cares?) to have any real impact.

First admit the truth about cigarette smoking; then go on to the consequences — the coughing, hawking, horrible aftertaste, hangover, dependency, inconvenience, expense, and social outcast status, and that is even before you start on the illnesses and cancers.

Thus also with drug education. First admit the attractions. Also tell the truth that some people can dabble and not go any further, though a drug like heroin is notoriously more addictive than a drug like ecstasy. Discuss addiction, or dependency, and the kind of people who might be vulnerable to it. Some experts, such as Dr Robert Lefever at the Promis Clinic in London, believe that addiction is genetically linked: you inherit a genetic predisposition to the syndrome, but this is not yet proven. (Will Self, the author, says "drug addiction is not a disease — it's a syndrome. It's a matrix of things: it is maladaptive behaviour, general and collective.")

There is no consensus on the question of whether the disposition to be addicted is inherited or not. It is certainly agreed that the more widely available a commodity becomes the more addicts will emerge. There must be potential alcoholics in Saudi Arabia but they have not had the opportunity to develop their addiction. But how much can, and should, society try to control an individual's behaviour? These are deeper questions which also need to be probed within the context of drug education. Certainly, just giving young people horror stories, or bombarding them with anti-drug propaganda does not work. One authoritative source, Raymond Goldberg, in a standard textbook claims that "drug education has had little effect on behaviour", except that it stimulates curiosity. A well-known campaign against heroin — "Heroin Screws You Up" — actually got more people interested in trying heroin.

If drug education is not working particularly well, we have to ask in what way it can be done better. With drugs, as with sex, a logical and rational approach is not enough. You have to realise that decisions in these matters are not always taken by the rational mind; and you have to relate the material to wider social issues and practices. The Dutch are (relatively) successful with sex education not because they teach high theory or press condoms on the young; they are candid about the consequences of too-early sex, but they also have a society in which young people are highly supervised, and seldom left to their own devices. They also have a relatively high numbers of mothers at home: Dutch culture is relentlessly domestic. Drug and sex education have to be socially contextual — they have to be related to the values within the society, which is, incidentally, why one size will not fit all within the diversity of European cultures.

When we educate about drugs, it seems to me, we have to be aware of the fact that we live in a drug culture in which we are all collaborators. Most drug deaths, and even drug addictions, are not just heroin, or cocaine, or speedballs: they are polydrug deaths. Ireland, in particular, has a serious polydrug problem. "Benzos" — benzodiazepine tranquillisers are widely and multiply abused. So are paracetamol and aspirin. The melancholy roll-call of drug-related deaths in the Dublin coroner's office repeatedly underlines polydrug use and abuse.

It is valid to have resort to medication for people in sickness, but our culture has hugely widened the concept of illness. We are absolutely wedded to the idea that there is "a pill for every ill". All heroin users say that the hardest thing about using is not stopping the habit; it is staying stopped. And while they are struggling to stay stopped, all around them the message reverberates that there is no necessity for anyone ever to suffer any pain or discomfort. A pill for every ill. Advertisers blare it — "got a headache? Reach for Nurofen!" — and many doctors pro-actively support this over-reliant legal drug culture. A woman, aged forty, loses her father, aged seventy-five. A bereavement is nearly always a sad occasion, but at the age of forty it is neither unnatural nor unexpected to lose a parent. What does her doctor say? Suggest a course of tranquillisers.

A man, aged forty-eight, loses his job. Not a nice thing to happen at any age, but perhaps especially difficult in mid-life crisis. He is depressed. So he is prescribed anti-depressants. Anti-depressants can be very effective for those with serious, clinical depression: I am not suggesting they be ruled out. But it doesn't need to be the first remedy in any given life crisis.

Got a sex problem? Take Viagra. Indeed, it is considered intolerable now to deny anyone the chance of constant sexual fulfilment, by "discriminating" against any supplicant for subsidised Viagra. Too shy to go into company? Consider Seroxat, the "anti-shyness" pharmaceutical.

Prozac (fluoxine), the "happiness drug" which produces chemical endomorphins in the brain has been taken by over eleven million people. Ritalin, the drug which controls Attention Deficient Disorder and hyperactivity in children, is another apparently very effective pharmaceutical, and about 6 per cent of American schoolchildren are now using it.

The contraceptive pill is a very effective drug which has been used, now, for forty years: in Britain, about ten per cent of 16-year-old girls are taking this chemical suppressant of fertility. At the other end of the reproductive spectrum, Hormone Replacement Therapy is the current wonderdrug for women entering, and experiencing, the menopause. Alcoholism is increasingly treated with the drug Naltraxone; there are hopes that heroin addiction may be treated with another drug now in development, Acamprosate, a partner to Naltraxone. A pill for every ill and a drug for every drug abuse.

Pharmaceuticals have played a very remarkable part in the treatment of a variety of illness, including mental illnesses such a schizophrenia, which was horribly stigmatised until effective drug treatment was discovered. But we have moved beyond using pharmaceuticals just for illness, we prescribe them to confront the problems of existence itself. "To be or not to be," asked Hamlet, in his own existential anguish. "That is the question." There are no answers to some of life's most anguishing questions. Sometimes, we just have to live with our pain. I think that, too, should be part of drug education: sometimes life will be very, very painful, very fearful, very sad. But we grow stronger and braver through the experience of it.

When we are practising the "pill for every ill" response, we are, in whatever small way, facilitating and endorsing the same habit as heroin. Heroin is the greatest "pill for any ill" of all time. In that, it is simply the logical extension of the comfort culture, the culture which will tolerate no pain, and considers happiness and well-being a right. When recovering heroin addicts tell Pauline Bissett, at the Broadway Lodge clinic in Somerset, that they have a headache, she suggests — to their surprise —

that they take a warm bath, or walk in the garden, or have a herbal tea. If it persists and becomes unbearable, yes, there is a place for medication, but do not automatically reach for a chemical substance for any discomfort.

This is the counter-cultural idea today: stoicism. If we really wanted to combat the power of heroin we would actively promote a revival of stoicism. We would teach that there are some difficulties, some discomforts and some distress you have to accept. We would also, perhaps, do something to contradict the promises that globalised capitalism, by its nature, endlessly makes: of instant success, instant gratification and instant excitement as the daily fare of the ordinary citizen.

In Oliver James's book *Britain on the Couch*, which he subtitled *Why we're unhappier than we were in the 1950s — despite being richer*, he claims that the alarming increase in suicide, especially among young males, since the 1960s is partly due to the impossibly high expectations of life today. The high expectations and stressful social conditions which go with competitive material striving are causing a drop in natural serotonin levels — serotonin being the natural chemical which produces the "feelgood factor" in human brains. And that is one of the reasons why people reach for a chemical high — because the *joie de vivre* of simpler times has been somehow diminished by consumer-led development.

In Ireland, in particular (and probably in Scotland too), there is another contributory cause to the increase in drug abuse: and that is in the decline in religion. Between 1980 and the end of the 1990s, the Republic of Ireland changed from being an intensely Catholic country to an increasingly secular society. The devotional magazines chart this change by observing, for example, the decline (starting in the 1970s) of family prayer, and the huge falloff, in the 1980s, of younger people going to church.

Irish Catholicism has often been characterised as "authoritarian" — well, most social systems were — but it was also intensely, even sensually passionate. The rites and rituals of traditional Catholicism were rich in psychic experience: Sean O'Faoilain remembered how, as a child he was regularly brought to kiss the gaudy statue of Jesus, Mary and John at Calvary. The poet Austin Clarke recalled, in the 1950s, the sheer intensity of the prayers. "O most adorable, precious and infinitely tender Heart pierced for the love of me, pierce my heart with the love of Thee ... Sacred Heart, I put my trust in thee, inflame my heart with Thy love ...."

In the Sean O'Casey slums of Dublin — now called less poetically, "the deprived inner city" — the soothing mantra of the rosary has been replaced by the soothing ingestion of Valium. And the prayer cycles which often confronted suffering, such as the Stations of the Cross — have given way to the nostrums of prozac or television escapism. Drugs, I believe, fill a space left by the moral vacuum, and the ritualistic vacuum. A Dutch anthropologist, Jean-Paul Grund, has suggested that the heroin culture is a replacement for ritual, because it becomes itself a deeply ritualised way of life, of acting out dramas which need some form of behavioural expression. There may even be, in the heroin cult, a submerged desire for suffering.

Marx famously wrote that "religion is the opium of the people". In Ireland today, he might well claim that "opium is the opium of the people". The lowest rate of weekly Mass attendance in Dublin is in Tallaght, West Dublin, which is one of the poorest, and most drug-afflicted, areas of the city.

211

We search for an overall solution to the drug problem; but there may not be any "overall solution". And there may be more differences of approach in the coming times too. It is possible that some societies will move towards a more liberal view of drug use, and a view of "the right to choose" even on abuse. The individualist notion that it is a person's entitlement to do what they choose with their own body has gained much ground in our time. The idea that the state, or the Government, should police or patrol individual choices is losing ground.

But if there is a model for resisting and opposing drug use, and a drug culture, it must surely lie with the great temperance movements of the nineteenth and early twentieth century. These movements, which were strong both in Britain and in Ireland (though in different ways) were profoundly democratic, often socialist in tone, spiritual and what we would call "empowering" to all kinds of disempowered groups.

I found an inspiring book in the public library in Kensington, London, called *The Dictionary of British Temperance*, which simply lists the men and women who went around the country giving public talks, often from personal experience, about temperance in the mid-Victorian period. They were often people who had had hard lives, sometimes being injured in mining or mill accidents. They had lived rough, and taken solace from the cheap gin available to the poor. But they turned around their lives through a personal commitment to temperance; and abstinence from intoxication became a new source of meaning, joy and achievement. These are extremely touching stories, and the temperance movements underpinned the foundation of the Labour party in England (and Sinn Fein, in its idealistic, 1905 manifestation in Ireland).

The temperance movement on this side of the Atlantic did not advocate prohibition (though they did sometimes come into conflict with the drink producers): but the overall emphasis was on the individual making a personal commitment, and on the group advocating virtue, not law. Temperance was also at its most effective with a spiritual dimension. The Pioneer Movement in Ireland, which crusaded against the abuse of alcohol, operated through this system of personal renunciation, for the greater good. Narcotics Anonymous is, in its own way, the heir to these great enterprises and the way in which this organisation is now flourishing, and attracting so many energetic and idealistic young people is by far the most optimistic pointer to the future of living sober and living free.

*

Strangely, it is almost as though I grew closer to my nephews after their deaths. I thought about them much more than I had during their lifetimes: you just take people for granted until they are gone. Then you are filled with remorse and regret for not seizing the day when it was there. I kept remembering little episodes from their lives; I'd wake up one morning and remember "Poor". "Poor" was a teddy-bear that Conor loved as a child, so called because he was "Poor Teddy". I was full of guilt for the way I had purchased a sweater for PK for Christmas. I had bought it in the Kilkenny Shop, making a special proviso that he would not exchange it for money, for fear it would go on the drug. When I thought of his life, I knew he must have suffered many regrets because that is part of the torment of being a drug user (and an alcohol user). If only there had been time to say that all, all can be redeemed, and all, all will be redeemed.

Everyone in the family kept dreaming about these precious young men. My most striking dream occurred in May 1999, just five months after that terrible Christmas. It was one of those vivid dreams which stays with you all through the next day. I was somehow informed that PK and Conor were, after all, alive. "They are not dead, but sleepeth." Patrick's eyes were seen to flicker and open, and he came to: I embraced him and knew then it had all been a big mistake. "We'll never let that happen to you again," I said. "We must make sure everything is all right now." I could feel the warmth of his body, though it was thin. Then I saw Conor revive. Doctors were arriving to ensure that the recovery was properly managed. Conor began drinking a can of beer. "Don't, darling," I said. "We must start afresh, with sobriety."

He smiled at me in that laughing way he had. The dream-film froze, and then faded.

Bibliography and Sources

Aeschbach, Ernst. *Heroin Distribution in Switzerland*. Schweizer Arzte gegen Drogen. 1998.

Barbaric, Father Slavo. *Pearls of the Wounded Heart. A religious approach to healing*. Medjugorje 1998.

Burroughs, William. *Naked Lunch*. First published, Olympia Press, Paris 1959. Flamingo Modern Classics, 1993.

Burroughs, William, *Junky*. First published in the US in 1953. Penguin Books UK 1977.

Booth Davies, John. *The Myth of Addiction*. Harwood Academic Publishers. 1997.

De Quincey, Thomas. *Confessions of an English Opium Eater*. First published, 1821: Penguin Classics 1971

Dixon, Patrick. *The Truth about Drugs*. Hodder & Stoughton, 1998

Dorn, Nicholas, et al. *Coping With a Nightmare: Family Feelings about Long-Term Drug Use*. Institute for the Study of Drug Dependence. London. Revisied edition 1994.

EMCCDDA (European Monitoring Centre for Drugs and Drug Addiction): *Evaluating Drug Prevention in the European Union*. Luxembourg — Office for Official Publications of the European Communities. 1998

EMCCDDA: *Annual report on the state of the drugs problem in the European Union*, 1998.

Francis, Paul. *Help Your Kids Stay Drug-Free*. Harper Collins 1999.

Fernandez, Humberto. *Heroin*. Hazelden, Minnesota. 1998.

Faulpel, Charles E. *Career Patterns of Hard-Core Heroin Users*. University of Florida Press 1991.

Fukuyama, Francis. *The Great Disruption*. Profile Books 1999.

Garratt, Sheryl. *Adventures in Wonderland: A Decade of Club Culture*. Headline 1998.

Gillett, Charlie. *The Sound of the City: The Rise of Rock and Roll*. Souvenir Press, 1983.

Goldberg, Ramond. *Taking Sides: Drugs & Society*. 3rd Edition. Dushkin/McGraw-Hill, Guilford, Conn. 1998.

Grund, Jean-Paul. *Drug Use as a Social Ritual. Functionality, Symbolism and Determinations of Self-Regulation*. IVO (Addiction Research Institute) Netherlands. 1993.

Haining, Peter (Ed.) *The Hashish Club: An Anthology of Drug Literature*. Peter Owen. 1975.

Hayter, Alathea. *Opium and the Romantic Imagination*. Faber and Faber, 1968.

Hewison, Robert. *Too Much. Art and Society in the Sixties: 1960-1975*. Methuen 1986.

Hunt, Marsha (Ed.). *The Junk Yard: Voices from an Irish Prison*. Mainstream Publishing, Edinburgh and London. 1999.

Hutchinson, R. High Sixties: *The Summers of Riot and Love*. Edinbrugh. Mainstream 1992.

James, Oliver. *Britain on the Couch: Treating a Low Serotonin Society*. Arrow Books 1998.

Kay, James and **Cohen**, Julian. *The Parents' Complete Guide to Young People and Drugs*. Vermillion. London 1998.

Kent, Nick. *The Dark Stuff: Selected Writings on Rock Music, 1972-1993*. Penguin Books 1994.

Kohn, Marek. *Narconmania: On Heroin*. Faber 1987.

Lyman, Michael D & **Potter**, Gary W. *Drugs in Society*. Anderson Publishing. Cincinnati 1991.

Marwick, Arthur. *The Sixties*. OUP 1998.

McFadyean, Melanie. *Drugs Wise: A Practical Guide for Concerned Parents about the Use of Illegal Drugs*. Icon Books, 1997.

Macken, Ultan. *Drug Abuse in Ireland*. Mercier Press, 1975.

Marks, Howard. *Mr Nice*. Vintage Books 1998.

Mitterauer, Michael. *A History of Youth*. Basil Blackwell, 1992.

O'Brien, Robert, et al. *Encyclopaedia of Drug Abuse: Facts on File*, New York and Oxford 1992.

Pike, Jeff. *The Death of Rock 'n' Roll. Untimely Demises ... in Pop Music*. Faber and Faber, 1993.

Platt, Jerome L. *Heroin Addiction Theory, Research and Treatment*, Krieger, Malabar, USA. 1995.

Pownall, M. *Face the Facts: Heroin*. Oxford: Heneimann Educational Books 1991.

Ruggiero, V et al. *Drug Use: Markets and Trafficking in Europe*. London. UCL Press. 1995.

Reynolds, Paul. *King Scum: The Life and Crimes of Tony Felloni, Dublin's Heroin Boss*. Gill & Macmillan 1998.

Self, Will. *Junk Mail*. Penguin Books 1996.

Shapiro, H. *Waiting for the Man*. London Quartet 1988.

Standing Conference on Drug Abuse (Ed.) *Drug Problems — Where to Get Help. A Comprehensive Guide to Drug Treatment and Care Services in England and Wales*. SCODA, Loman St, London SE 1 OEE.

Stoppard, Miriam. *Drugs Info File: From Alcohol & Tobacco to Ecstasy & Heroin*. Dorling Kindersley, 1999.

Sweet, Corinne. *Overcoming Addiction*. Piatkus 1994.

Trebach, Arnold S. *The Heroin Solution*. Yale Univeristy Press. 1982.

Tyler, Andrew. *Street Drugs*. Coronet Books, 1986. Revised edition, 1995.

Stewart, Tam. *The Heroin Users*, Pandora. 1987.

Welsh, Irvine. *The Acid House*. Vintage 1995.

Williams, Paul. *The General*. The O'Brien Press. Dublin 1998.

Williams, Paul. *Gangland*. The O'Brien Press, Dubin 1998.

Youngson, Robert M. *Prescription Drugs*. HarperCollins. 1994.

Zoja, Luigi. *Drugs, Addiction and Initiation*. Sigo Press, Boston. (No date given.)

Papers and Journals:

Addiction Counselling World: ACW, London SW 1V YU. Miscellaneous issues.

Best, David et al. *Continued heroin use during methadone treatment: relationships between frequency of use and reasons reported for heroin use. Drug and Alcohol Dependence* 53 (1999) 191-5 National Addiction Centre, 4 Windsor Walk, Denmark Hill, London SE 5 8AF.

Brown, Roy et al. 'Sexual Abuse in childhood and subsequent illicit drug abuse in adolescence and early adulthood.' *Irish Journal of Psychiatric Medicine 1998*. 15: 4.

Byrne, Ray. 'The relative mortality risks of Methadone and Other Drugs Implicated in Drug Related Deaths Investigated by the Dublin City Coroner in 1998.' Dissertation submitted to the Dublin Institute of Technology. April 1999.

Metribian, Nick et al. 'Feasibility of Prescribing Injectable Heroin and Methadone to Opiate-Dependent Drug Users: Associated Health Gains and Harm Reductions.' *Journal of the Australian Medical Association*. 15 June 1998.

O'Connor, et all. 'A Review of the Characteristics and Treatment Progress of 45 Prenan Opiate Addicts Attending the Irish National Drug Advistory and Treatment Centre Over a Two Year Period.' *Irish Journal of Medical Science*. Vol. 157, No 5. May 1988.

Rooney, S et al. 'Co-Abuse of Opiates and Benzodiazepines.' *Irish Journal of Medical Science,* Vol 168. No 1. Jan-March 1999.

The Shrew Magazine: 'The Truth About Drugs in Ireland.' November/December 1998.

Heroin: The Ultimate Challenge. Papers from conference on heroin held at Regents College, London on 14 July 1999. Release.

Helplines

There is a growing number of organisation and addiction centres offering help and rehabilitation. A fuller list is available from the regional health boards.

Irish Republic

Narcotics Anonymous: 086-8629308.

Naranon: Family help. 01-874-8431.

Also: Alcoholics Anonymous, 109 South Circular Road Leonards Corner, Dublin 8. 01-453-8998.

Dublin: The National Drug Treatment Centre, Trinity Court, Pearse Street, Dublin 2. 01-677-1122.

The Merchant's Quay Project, 4 Merchant's Quay, Dublin 2. 01-679-0044. 01-677-1128.

Anna Liffey Drug Project, 13 Lower Abbey Street Dublin 1. 01-878-6899

Aisling Clinic, Cherry Orchard Hospital, Ballyfermot, Dublin 10. Tel: 01-623-2200/620-6010.

Ballymun Youth Action Project, 1a Balcurris Road, Ballymun. Dublin 11. 01-842-8071.

Teach Mhuire Rehabilitation, 38 Lower Gardiner Street Dublin 1. 01-878-8877.

EURAD: Information and Advice, 3, Haigh Terrace, Dun Laoghaire Co Dublin . Tel: 01-284-1164 E-mail: eurad@iol.ie

Arbour House Treatment Centre, St Finbar's Hospital, Douglas Road, Cork 021-968933

Addiction Counselling Service, Day Hospital, 7 Dublin Road, Tuam, Co. Galway. 093-24695

Community Addiction Counselling Services, Mental Health Centre, Mountbellow, Co Galway. 0905-79571

St Loman's Hospital, Mullingar, Co. Westmeath. 044-40191

Alcohol and Drug Counselling Services, 1, Coote Terrace, Portlaoise, Co. Laoise. 0502-21364. ext. 409

St Anne's Day Hospital, Addiction counselling, Roxboro
   Road, Limerick. 061-315177
Bushypark Treatment Centre, Ennis, Co Clare.
   065-684-0944
Alcohol and Substance Counselling, North Western
   Health Board, 12 Johnson Court, Sligo. 071-43316.
Waterford Drug Helpline: 051-37 33 33

Northern Ireland

The National Drugs Helpline for Britain is also
   operative in Northern Ireland. 0800-77-66-00.
AA in Northern Ireland, 152 Lisburn Road, Belfast BT 9
   6AJ. 08-01232-681084
Carlisle House, Henry Place, Belfast 15.
   08-01232-328308.
Research Group on Chemical Dependency, Graham
   House, 1-5 Albert Square, Belfast BT 1 3EQ.
   08-01232-240900.
Community Addiction Team in Ballymena have a
   comprehensive list of helping services throughout
   Northern Ireland. 08-01266-658462

Britain

National Drugs Helpline covers the whole of the UK
   and Northern Ireland.
Narcotics Anonymous: 0171-730-0009
Families Anonymous: 0171-498-4680
AA Central Office for England and Wales, General
   Service Office of AA P.O., Box 1, Stonebow House,
   York, YO1 2NJ. 01904-644026.
AA for Scotland, Baltic Chambers, 50 Wellington Street,
Glasgow, G2 6HJ. 0141-2219027
Standing Conference on Drug Abuse provides
   comprehensive advice on all drug services with
   detailed guides of local drug units throughout the
   UK

SCODA, 32-36 Loman Street, London SE1 OEE. 0171-928-9500.

The Institute for the Study of Drug Dependence (ISDD) has an excellent library service and comprehensive archive on drug research. It sells publications on behalf of other organisations, including all European Community publications.

ISDD 32-36 Loman Street London SE 1 OEE Tel 0171-928-1211.

There is a network of drug helplines throughout the European Community, available from the European Foundation of Drug Helplines (FESAT). 19 Rue du Marteau, 1000 Bruxelles, Belgique. Tel (32) 2 219 28 87. Fax (32) 2 219 1498. Email: FESATbureau@csi.com